*rom Jenny*

letters from **Jenny**

EDITED AND INTERPRETED BY
GORDON W. ALLPORT

AN ORIGINAL HARBINGER BOOK

HARCOURT, BRACE & WORLD, INC.
New York   Chicago   Burlingame

Library of Congress Catalog Card Number: 65–18327

PRINTED IN THE UNITED STATES OF AMERICA

M N O P

ISBN 0-15-650700-5

preface

Intimate letters, gushing forth from raw personal experience, have a unique fascination. Often better than fiction or biography, even than autobiography, they tell us what a particular concrete human life is like. The fascination is greater if the letters are written over a considerable period of time, presenting consecutively the inner narrative of a life as it unfolds.

The Letters of Jenny Gove Masterson tell the story of a mother–son relationship and trace the course of a life beset by frustration and defeat. At the same time they reveal in Jenny a vivid, indeed a dramatic, personality. Although she herself is a lover of literature, Jenny seems unaware that she possesses literary talent. Her ability to set forth her perceptions and her feelings is fired by hot necessity, unmonitored by self-consciousness.

Between the ages of fifty-eight and seventy she wrote a series of 301 letters to two young friends, a married couple living and teaching in an eastern college town. The tie of friendship extended back to the time when the husband (Glenn) had been the roommate of Jenny's son (Ross) at college, about ten years before the beginning of the correspondence. During these ten years there was no consecutive exchange of letters—none at all for a period of six years. The correspondence begins in earnest in March, 1926, and continues without interruption for eleven and a half years, until Jenny's death in October, 1937.

Fortunately Glenn and his wife (Isabel) preserved all her letters. Sensing their potential psychological value they made them available for editing, for analysis, and for publication. To me they seemed to have special promise as case material in teaching theories of personality. Accordingly, I undertook the task and in 1946 published the Letters in two consecutive issues of the *Journal of Abnormal and Social Psychology* (Volume 41, Nos. 3 and 4).

The names of all persons and of all places (excepting only New York and Chicago) are fictitious or disguised. For purpose of publication the Letters have been abridged to approximately one-third their original length. Some are reproduced in full, some altogether omitted. I have, however, made a special effort to preserve the original proportion of subject matter. I should add that Glenn, while visiting Jenny shortly before her death, asked whether she would be willing sometime in the future to have her letters published. Although surprised by the request she replied with characteristic incisiveness, "Yes, if you think they would do anybody any good." For nearly two decades the Letters have done "good," proving their value as teaching material.

Speaking for myself I may say that I have found the Letters the most effective case material I have ever encountered for provoking fruitful class discussions of theories of personality. I have sometimes asked myself why they should be so stimulating and pedagogically so effective. Much credit must go to Jenny and her flair for clear and forceful expression of her perceptions and feelings. But there is a deeper reason. Every male reader is himself a son; every female reader is a mother or a potential mother. Therefore the bitter dilemma of Ross and his mother often seems to echo the reader's own personal (but usually milder) problem. Like a Greek tragedy the Letters have a universal appeal.

In Part I of this volume there appears first a brief statement of the background of Jenny's life before the age of fifty-eight. The Letters then follow, precisely as she wrote them, save for the abridgment. Occasional statements concerning important happenings are inserted in the text in order to clarify the allusions in the letters. At two points letters from Jenny's son, Ross, appear. These are the only cues that we have concerning Ross's view of his mother's personality. Whether or not the reader accepts Ross's interpretation of the relationship, his letters provide a valuable perspective on Jenny's narrative.

For many years I have been interested in the use of personal documents by psychological science, especially for the light they shed on theories of personality. Elsewhere I have discussed the matter at some length (*The Use of Personal Documents in Psychological Science.* New York: Social Science Research Council, Bulletin No. 49, 1942). For our present purpose, however, I shall call attention to only a few important features of letters which, it should be noted, are only one class of personal documents (diaries, autobiographies, and questionnaires representing other types).

Psychologists have rarely made a close analysis of letters. The reasons are not far to seek. In the first place long series of personal letters are hard to come by. The original recipient is likely to destroy them one by one as they are received and read, or else to guard them from prying eyes (especially perhaps of psychologists). Even when, in rare cases, they are made available they often turn out to be too stilted for use, yielding little more than a recital of humdrum happenings. Sometimes the opposite fault exists: a self-conscious smartness reflecting little more than the author's brand of verbal exhibitionism.

There is an additional handicap. It takes two people to sustain a correspondence, and seldom are both sets of letters available. Even when available the exchange may reflect primarily the development of an interpersonal relationship, thus telling more about the dyadic situation (perhaps a developing love affair) than about the personality of either writer.

Sceptics argue further that in letters a writer tells only what he consciously knows. His unconscious motives are hidden from him and therefore from the reader. To this serious objection a rejoinder is possible: the writer's style of expression, his juxtaposition of ideas, what lies between the lines—all aid in reconstructing the unconscious portions of the writer's mental life. But the criticism cannot lightly be brushed aside. Since it runs into the deepest depths of psychological controversy we shall explore it more fully in Part II of this volume.

All these objections taken together show that the limitations of letters as psychological case material are very real and help to explain why so little professional use has been made of them.

Jenny's Letters, however, escape most of the common faults. She writes fluently, with a naturally brilliant literary style, and with little self-consciousness. Ingenuously she tells of her interests, hates, fears, and conflicts. Her uninhibited expression seems to challenge the reader to reconstruct the themes and personal mechanisms of which she herself is only partially aware.

Especially important is the fact that her relationship with her correspondents (Glenn and Isabel) remains essentially static. That is to say, what they wrote to Jenny does not alter the relationship, nor does it affect the flow of her narrative. Jenny wanted a pair of sympathetic listeners. Without their ears her solitude would have been unbearable. And so for eleven years they served as a projection screen upon which Jenny displayed the story of her hopes, jealousies, striving, and defeat. Although they replied to her letters, sent gifts, and occasionally visited her, they made no effective attempt to alter the life-drama being enacted before them. Indeed, they were powerless to do so.

To me the principal fascination of the Letters lies in their challenge to the reader (whether psychologist or layman) to "explain" Jenny—if he can. Why does an intelligent lady behave so persistently in a self-defeating manner? When and how might she have averted the tragedy of her life? Could proper guidance or therapy at an appropriate time have helped alter the rigid course of her conduct? Was the root of her trouble some wholly unconscious mechanism? If so, what was its nature? The dynamics of Jenny's life are deeply puzzling. They invite the reader to test his own insight and apply where relevant his knowledge of human nature.

And one may ask, Do ordinary psychological rubrics adequately fit Jenny's case? One might label her as hysterical, overprotective, aggressive, asocial, extropunitive, an isolate, paranoid, having a character disorder. But do these categories singly or in combination represent the focal dispositions of her unique being?

Whatever else Jenny may be she is extraordinarily expressive. The reader easily loses himself in the uninhibited flow of her feelings and perceptions, so much so that he is likely to forget that expressivity is itself a core feature of personality. *Le style est l'homme même.* The sample of her handwriting here reproduced seems to confirm the impression of fluency, clarity, and forcefulness that mark her entire personality.

viii lovely room for $1.50. No religion about it — Just business, No hypocrisy — they had a bed to sell — I rented it — that's all.

I never intended to sponge on anyone in Canada — I meant to live on my own money long as it lasted & when it was all gone to step out of the picture. That is what I must do here, Intend to do. And why not? Who cares? Of what use am I to anyone on Earth? This coming back to prison gives me a chance to destroy things I love, & meant to use in Canada, Some photographs, & a few more books, I will "get my house in order" without delay, already the extreme weariness & tension has left my body, or nearly so — I can think once more, Merciful Heaven, what a tremendous hold I must have on what we call life — My mother must have been a healthy woman, Best love to you all — more later

Lady B.

Psychologists are on safe ground so long as they talk in abstractions about personality-in-general. Their real test comes when they attempt to explain (or guide or therapeutically treat) a single concrete life. In reflecting on the case of Jenny I find myself wishing that I could take refuge in vague generalizations, but invariably she pins me down with the unspoken challenge, "And what do you make of *me?*"

And so, aware as I am of my audacity, I make bold to present this edition of the Letters, together with extended analytical comments in Part II. I do so because I know of no other case material so rich and exciting and challenging for those who like to explore the mysteries of human nature, whether they be students of psychology or devotees of literature or simply observers of life.

G. W. A.

Cambridge, Massachusetts
November, 1964

contents

letters from Jenny

part one. the *L*etters

chapter one. *Jenny's background*

Since the letters cover only the final years of Jenny's life, it is necessary for the reader to have in mind an outline of events up to the point where the correspondence begins.

Born in Ireland, of Protestant parentage, in 1868, Jenny lived her first five years on a large estate where her father was chief caretaker and her mother the principal of a small school. The family migrated to Canada in 1873, the parents establishing their new home in Montreal. Here Jenny lived with her five younger sisters and one younger brother until she was 27 years old.

Although the family identified themselves with the Scotch-English culture of their community, the mother by her rich store of songs and stories kept alive the love of Irish lore in the transplanted family. She was domestically a competent woman as well as outstanding in her scholarly tastes, and assisted the children in obtaining as good an education as was possible. But when Jenny was 18 her father died and she had to leave school to find employment to help support her younger sisters and brother. She became a telegrapher and for nine years continued in this work in Montreal.

By the time Jenny was 27 her siblings were married or self-supporting, so she was relieved of all responsibility toward the family. Though reverencing her mother's memory and sharing especially her ideals of education and cultivation, she found little in common with her brother and sisters. They were conservative;

she rebellious. They adhered closely to the Church of England; she read and agreed with Tom Paine. They participated in the rather dull and circumscribed social life of the neighborhood; she preferred to take long walks alone and to read books in solitude. Instead of marrying a man who would fit into the conservative Gove pattern of life, she married an American railway inspector, a Henry Masterson. Because he had been divorced from his first wife, her brother and sisters, close adherents of the English Church, considered this marriage, as did the Church at that time, a family disgrace. After a bitter quarrel Jenny broke her connection with the family for a period of seven years.

Moving to Chicago with her husband, Jenny found it irksome to remain idle all day in their small flat. She was accustomed to earning her own living, and in recalling these days tells how sometimes in the morning she would find she had put on her hat to go to work before she became aware that she no longer had a job. She complained that she felt she was being "kept" by a man. She quarreled more than once with her husband over this issue, but he, like most men of his day, was firmly set against a wife seeking employment. Before this problem was settled, Mr. Masterson died. A month or so later their son, Ross, was born. That was in 1897; Jenny was 29 years of age.

She had spent extravagantly to care for Mr. Masterson in his last illness; it was now necessary to return to work as a telegrapher to support herself and infant son. She did not complain of widowhood but was well satisfied to have a child for whom she might work and to whom she might devote her undivided affection. So long as Ross was small she kept him with her in a small apartment adjoining the telegraph office in Ohio where she was sole operator. She was so content with this arrangement that she rejected two or three desirable offers of marriage.

When Ross was five years old she returned to Montreal with him on a holiday visit to her sisters. They proposed that Ross stay for a few months with his cousins while his mother returned to Ohio. He adapted well, outgrew many of his "spoiled" ways, such as food capriciousness, but on her return Jenny accused her sisters of neglecting him and starving him. They in turn accused her of spoiling Ross, but heard her retort that she would gladly scrub floors so that he could have a pony. And so, once more in a quarrel, she parted from them, severing relations this time for twenty-five years.

Later she placed Ross in an expensive boarding school in Chicago, taking a position as librarian in a large mercantile concern in that city. A lover of books, she found this work to her taste. But it paid little more than enough to cover the expenses of her son's school and costly summer camp. She regimented herself with the strictest economy. Her diet was chiefly cereal and milk. Her room was windowless, a kind of linen room in a large apartment house. Ross called her his "swallow who lives in a flue." Through rigid, but glad, self-denial she provided her son with every advantage. His schools were the most select. She purchased for him beautifully bound classics and taught him to love good literature, especially the Irish poets, and to appreciate the exhibitions at the Art Institute. She gave him special drawing lessons and saved money for college.

For a philosophy of life she offered him Tom Paine, Schopenhauer, and Omar Khayyam. She assured him that apart from art and natural beauties it was a miserable world to live in, and that it was her duty to sacrifice for him in every way since she was responsible to him for his existence. She also told him that he owed her no debt of gratitude. Though Ross accepted all of this philosophy and teaching readily enough, he did not apply it immediately; his companionship with her continued close and congenial. Their talks together were endless and intimate, their tastes much alike.

Physically Ross resembled his mother with his raven-black hair, flashing eyes, and tall, sturdy body. Both were handsome, Irish in type, aristocratic and fastidious in their tastes, immaculately clean, neat in dress. To the day of her death Jenny's skin was unwrinkled, a soft ivory. Her eyes were gray-green and her mouth mobile and strongly molded. She dressed conservatively and in black. Ross had never seen his mother in anything but black, she said. Some thought her appearance and bearing a trifle mannish. She always wore a band of black ribbon around her throat and was never seen without an old-fashioned gold pin with the

Hebrew benediction Mizpah in raised gold letters. Mr. Masterson had given it to her on their wedding day.

Until Ross was 17 he and his mother were the closest of companions. She became headmistress of a girls' dormitory near the school Ross attended so that they might spend their free time together. Fully satisfied with one another's company, they had few friends. After preparatory school Ross went east to college while his mother resumed her librarianship in Chicago. Because of its twin ideals of scholarship and gentlemanliness, Princeton was their choice. Jenny returned gladly to her rigid routine of economy, and paid promptly any and all of Ross's bills, keeping him sufficiently supplied with spending money so that he might be at no disadvantage among his classmates. She wished him to live like a gentleman.

Ross was ending his sophomore year when the United States entered World War I. In the summer of 1917 he enlisted in the ambulance corps. Before he sailed for France his mother came east to say goodbye, and at that time met his college friends. She liked them all, particularly his roommate (to whom the correspondence is addressed); but she disliked his girl friends, and was particularly jealous of, and quarrelsome toward, an older woman, a professor's wife, whom she thought too attentive to her handsome son.

Returning from France in 1919, a member of the "lost generation," Ross found himself disoriented, badly adjusted to old scenes and old ambitions. But because of his mother's insistence he returned to college to complete work for his degree. Jenny again willingly resumed her responsibility for his expenses. After receiving his degree in 1921 he tried to make some business connection in New York City. Failing, he entered the Marines for a year. Still dissatisfied, he returned to New York, suggesting to his mother that she move east and find work in New York City. She did so, obtaining a clerical position which she held for three years. During these three years Ross was alternately employed and unemployed (as the opening letter tells). Quarrels with his mother about his women friends were frequent and bitter. During this period, in 1923, Ross married, keeping his marriage a secret from his mother. But she discovered the deception (through considerable detective work on her own), and her rage was mighty. On his first visit to her following her discovery she drove him out of her room with violent denunciations and a threat to have him arrested if he ever tried to see her again.

Feeling lost without her occasional, if tempestuous, contacts with her son, and feeling nostalgic too, no doubt, for the happy days of early college when, as she said, Ross was "all hers," she renewed her acquaintance with Ross's roommate whom she had liked when she met him some years before. In 1925 the roommate (Glenn) and his bride (Isabel) called on Jenny in her tiny room in New York. She entertained them graciously at a nearby restaurant (using for the purpose one of the ten-dollar bills she kept interleaved in an old magazine). She told them, in the vigorous language so characteristic of her, how Ross had deceived her, how she regarded him as a "cur" and how, so far as she was concerned, he was now "dead forever." She spoke of her poor health, saying that she suffered from abnormal heart action and enlargement of the heart, a condition carried over from childhood when she had been seriously ill, but for which she must have compensated in later years. She was always a tremendous walker and climbed towers and stairs unhesitatingly in spite of some pain. Her employment was not regular, but she flatly refused any offer of material aid. She merely wished to keep in touch with Glenn and Isabel to reduce her own feeling of loneliness. She was sentimentally pleased to have renewed this friendship of the pleasant past. They sometimes called her "Lady Masterson" and, accepting the playful title, she occasionally signed her letters with it.

For a year or so she kept up a polite but not intensive correspondence with Glenn and Isabel. Then deciding to cut short her New York sojourn, and to place herself beyond easy reach of her son should he try to find her, she returned to Chicago, from which city the first letter is written.

chapter two. 1926–1929

My dearest Glenn and Isabel:

There is a matter of considerable importance that worries me, and I earnestly desire you two children to discuss it with me, if you will be so very kind—and I feel sure that you will.

In order to make myself clear I must write you a series of letters—and I particularly request that you wait until you read the fourth letter before writing to me. The letters will be: 1. Ross. 2. New York. 3. Chicago. 4. The question. This is No. 1—Ross.

We were in New York—Ross roomed with an artist who had an apartment—I was in the cubby hole on 16th St. No heat, no window. Ross was out of employment. I was ill—dreadfully ill. I tried to work in fits and starts, my salary once so low as $14 a week, but I insisted on Ross's coming to my room often—2 or 3 times a week, and I cooked good porterhouse steaks for him, and bought him good cigars. I practically starved to do it. Weighed 96 lbs.

Then Ross found a position—he was quite delighted—it was such a good position, with fine prospects, salary $50 a week. He offered to cover my rent—$25 a month, and I said it would be a great help. He paid 1 month ($25.). The next

7

month slipped by until the 15th. My rent was due on the first. Ross said he was "rather pressed for money" and could only spare $20. I was stung to the quick, but took it. The 3rd month he was again late, but he offered me $25. He called at my room when I was out, and left the money, with a note.

I sent it back to him—said he evidently needed it worse than I and that I refused to accept anything at all from so niggardly a giver.

I got no more—he offered none. Six months slipped by—Ross lost his position and was again out of employment. He had little or no money and I again filled in the gap insisting on setting good meals, cigars, etc. When his tooth showed signs of decay I gave him $10. He failed to go to a Dentist, and believing he had used the money, I supplied another 10—I gave $30 for the Dentist, but he never had the tooth attended to. When he got that position in Brooklyn he wanted to go out there to room and asked me for *the loan* of 10. I emptied my purse that evening as we sat on my bed together, gave him my entire savings —$30 and kept 2.50 for myself to carry me over until my next pay. At that time I was receiving $18 a week.

It was in Brooklyn that he met the old maid with money who bought and married him. He never even mentioned money to me again. Never once offered to help me in any way.

I am a strongly intuitive person, am subject to impressions—beliefs—prejudices etc. not founded on any basis of reason.

It was my "feeling" for a long time that Ross was lying to me—when he said he could not come to see me because he was so very busy, I felt that he lied. When he spoke of his low salary I felt that he lied. Yet I was ashamed: I never tried to prove, or disprove, anything. I thought "the boy is all right— every word he says is probably true—it is I who am mean, suspicious, and hateful—forget it," and so the time went by.

The day he was married he said he could not keep his appointment with me to put up a shelf I needed because he had to stay at the store and help take inventory. I knew he lied that day, and was angry—I asked why should an efficiency man in a Dept. Store take inventory. He said it was mean of me to doubt him, and that all I had to do was telephone the 7th floor of the store an'd ask for him. He knew I would not do that. He ran his bluff—he just lied.

The last day I spent in New York before coming here, last September, I went to Jersey and saw the General Mgr. of the place where Ross had such splendid prospects. I wanted to know why Ross left, and what salary he had received. He left because they asked him to leave, his work was not satisfactory. He received $75 a week for 6 mos. $75. Think of it! I was starving on 14. Sick, so sick—in a room without heat—a bed without a blanket—no winter coat—weight 97 lbs. Think of it! Ross was too "hard pressed" for money to spare $25 a month, and gave only 20 and even that for only 2 months. And he received over *three hundred dollars a month* for *six months.*

When at the store only a very short time he borrowed from the Co. *$150.00* said he was married and his wife had to undergo an operation. He finally repaid the loan. He actually had the nerve to take to the office a sporting woman and her illegitimate child whom he introduced as his wife. The men laughed behind Ross's back for the woman was stamped, as they all are, and they knew he lied.

Ross brought this same woman and her brat to my house one Sunday evening and I was angry and told him that if he ever brought any more prostitutes to my house I would have them both arrested. Anyone, short of a fool, would know what she was at one glance.

This is my first letter (I am all trembling). My next will be No. 2—New York.

Au revoir,

Lady Masterson

Chicago, Ill. 3/12/26

My dearest Glenn and Isabel:

This is letter No. 2—New York. After Ross sold himself to the old maid buyer, and had reproached me for never having giving him *a home,* I fell into a panic-stricken condition which bordered closely on insanity. Altho' Ross had never at any period of his life been of any financial help to me, yet I felt that in case of real need he would stand by me and protect me. I had his address, telephone, etc. in a conspicuous place on my table, and carried them in my purse. You remember that my heart had become badly enlarged. I suffered from dizziness, and pain, and was told quite plainly by 2 or 3 Drs. that it would not be surprising if I dropped dead. Ross knew all this.

I had about $50. when Ross sold himself for a "home" and I was too dreadfully ill for anything. If I dropped dead on the street (and I often felt like it) no one would know who I was, as I had taken Ross's address from my purse. The $50 were in a Bank, but no one knew what Bank. I would be taken to the Morgue, not claimed, and be buried in Potter's Field, and in the meantime the money would lie useless, and unclaimed, in the Bank.

I saved and saved and soon had 2 or 3 fifties in the Bank. There was a woman in N. Y. whom I had known in a way, for several years. I liked her. I believed her to be a high-principled, understanding, splendid woman. I asked her if I might carry her name in my purse, and if, in case of need, she would see to it that I was cremated, not buried. She willingly promised, and I made a will in her favor, and I kept on saving.

After I visited my friend a few times, I found that my idol had, indeed, clay feet. She was quite an ordinary person. She had a man, quite an ordinary fellow, living with her in her apartment. In speaking of him to me she said "I do not need to tell *you* that ———— is not an intelligent man, but he is kind, and has money."

I felt as if the ground had slipped from under my feet. At once I saw that my friend was much too fat, her stomach like a sack, and she did not wear a corset. Her skirt was short as if she were 16 and her legs were big and coarse. Her arms like a ham. I almost hated her. If it were a romance, if those two only loved each other, if she thought him lovely, even if he possessed no lovely qualities—if he were clever and expressed high sentiments and splendid thoughts! But no. It was common and mean—no better than Ross who had sold his manhood and honor for "a home."

My awakening had a good deal to do with my leaving New York—I would go away altogether and break my connection with her—we can find prostitutes on any street corner.

And in the meantime she held my will, and if I dropped dead she could (and would) claim my money which I had starved to save, and the "Tennyson" which Mr. ——— gave me years and years ago, and my 6 silver spoons; and she could (and probably would) burn Isabel's wedding handkerchief, and my lovely little pig that is always here beside me on the table—and so that's the way.

I wrote to her early in January and asked her to send me the will. No reply—all January—all February. Early in March I wrote again, and she replied that she had mailed it to me several weeks ago. I did not say a word, but you may be sure that I do not believe her.

My next letter will tell of my experience in Chicago. It is to laugh—I am surely some hoo-doo'd lady; but still its possibly a good thing that those experiences have come to me at this time. That experience, and the one I shall write about in my next, have helped me to get my mental bearings—have taken me out of myself, and away from the horror of Ross's betrayal. I was forced to work, to keep going, and to *keep well,* in order to protect that money in the bank, and to finally save myself from those people.

Circumstances crowded on me—I would never have chosen them.

All during those years and years that I have lived as a hermit socially in order to pay the bills of that contemptible dog, I have never formed any social connection. I never had proper clothes—never had money to spare to entertain, even in a small way. And I *would not* be a sponge. My whole life has been wasted.

I shall write tomorrow if I can.

Au revoir.

Lady Masterson

Chicago, Ill. March 14/26

My dearest Glenn and Isabel:

This is letter No. 3—Chicago. It was in 1915 when Ross graduated from the Academy that I met Mrs. ———. She was employed by the same Co. in one of their office Depts. It happened we lived near each other, and so we met frequently on trains, etc. I never cared for the woman, she was coarse and vulgar, and loose in her dealings with men; but, of course, in the Library, I had to meet everyone in the house whether I liked them or not; however, we were never at all intimate until 1920 when Ross graduated, and I was to go East.

Now, I knew that this woman had affairs with men—even when her husband was alive and she was living with him, but you see that was in 1915, and we have all grown some older since then, and the woman's husband has died, and so maybe her affairs were really platonic as she claimed they were. Anyway, even if she were a bit "shady" she was no worse than my "friend" in N. Y.

Well, when I wrote about my intention of coming to Chicago she was profuse and strong in insisting that I must live with her. She said she had a 4 Rm. apt. and plenty of room, and that she was often lonely, and she would love to have me, etc. I had no intention of living with her and said so, but I said I would be glad to stay for a few days until I found a room, and so I came, and she met me at the train.

On the way up from the Depot to her apartment she told me that she did not live alone, that her "boy friend" lived with her, but that it would be all right, and I must make myself at home. I nearly fell dead. Needless to say that I hustled out without delay, and found this apartment, and moved in.

The "boy friend" stands 6 ft. 4 and weighs about 300 lbs. and he may have sense enough to go in out of the rain, but no one would ever suspect it by speaking to him. I did not quarrel with them of course. It is no affair of mine, and I don't care what they do, or how they live.

I consider that the woman had a con-

siderable nerve to suppose that I would have no objection to being a 3rd party in her love-nest, but I understand perfectly well
why she thought to trap me into living with her. The Co. that
employs her is strictly high class. If they dreamed for one moment that she was crooked they would dismiss her at once. They
all know me. I was employed by them for about 6 years, and so
this woman knew it would be a protection for her to have me in
the house.

My motive in coming to Chicago was not
governed to any extent by the fact that this woman lived here. I
came to Chicago because I know the city better than I know any
other city except New York. I never liked the place—do not like it
now—never liked it—but I have a business connection here, and
found a position without any delay at all.

It is hard work—extremely trying on one's
nerves—the Adjustment Dept. in a big Dept. Store—but my salary
went on almost without a break when I left N. Y. and that counts.

And then seeing all the old places almost
blotted Ross entirely from my mind, and that was my main object
in coming; the move was just what I needed. We have the most
beautiful Art Museum you could possibly imagine. N. Y. museum
is not a patch on it. The one here is a work of art. The one in
N. Y. is like a big gloomy prison—its high steep grand stairway of
grey stone that is almost perpendicular and seems to end in the
ceiling, gave me cold chills up my spine. The Chicago grand stairway is white marble—low broad steps—grand, broad landings with
sculpture on them. Old Voltaire in his chair on the first landing
has been there for over 20 years, and I almost wept for joy on
seeing him again. I used to carry Ross on my back when he was a
little fellow, and we knew every picture, and every group. To
hunt them all up, glad to see those I love, still there; sorry to miss
one here and there taken down, has all done me a world of good,
so that despite my friend's and her boy-friend's failure to supply
any of my real needs, my trip to Chicago was well taken.

There is one letter more.

Au revoir.

J. G. M.

Chicago, Ill., March 17/26

My dearest Glenn and Isabel:

This is my 4th, and last, letter, and will explain why I wrote the other 3. The one regarding Ross was not to show how contemptible Ross was, but to show how impossible it would be for me to ever again believe one word that left his lips—to ever trust him, or rely on him, to have the smallest faith in him.

The one about N. Y. was to show my effort to protect myself, and my lack of real friends in that City.

My Chicago experience is to show that I have accomplished what I aimed to do in making the trip, and as a result I do not need to remain here.

I have some money in a bank in Chicago, no one knows what bank, or how much, the book is held in the bank. I suffer from heart disease—my heart is enlarged. I can place my affairs in the hands of a Trust Co. and go on working in my present position, they have no intention at all of "letting me out," but my position is not worth keeping. For one thing, there's no money in it—only $20 a week. I work like a steam engine from 8 a.m. to 5.30. At Christmas time I nearly died. We worked from 8 to 6. Christmas-eve was a horror. Life under such conditions is not worth living. I must find a position where I have, at least, Saturday afternoon. Even less money, and not such a sledge-hammer job would suit me better. If I stay on here, I shall drop over my desk some day, and then what? Am I to be at the mercy of this woman (the Chicago woman) who sells her soul for food and drink

Will you—Glenn and Isabel—help me?

I do not mean to take me into your home, or be burdened with me at any time, but to handle my affairs, and protect me. My plan is this:—To make a will—I shall always have money enough to cover my expenses—there's enough in the bank at this moment to cremate me half a dozen times. If I drop dead the City would notify Glenn, and Glenn would authorize them to have me placed in an inexpensive coffin, and cremated.

He could do that by telegraph—no need to make a trip anywhere. I had Mr. Masterson cremated here in Chicago, and I think it only cost $30. He was taken from the Undertakers to the Cemetery —no fuss—no having mourning around. Only a foolish person would put money into a casket that is to be burned up the next day. Then Glenn could draw my money from the bank, and cover expenses. I have trifling treasures I would like to leave to Isabel. If I became ill, Glenn would have to telegraph the authorities to have me placed in an inexpensive—or free—ward—and say I have no property, or means. Let the City support me for a while (I have paid high rents for a long time). When one is ill it makes no difference what sort of a ward one is in, so long as its clean—and they are all clean. It is when one is convalescent that one needs a little money, and comforts. That is where my bank account should come in.

By the time I am old enough to enter an Old Ladies Home I shall have plenty of money to cover my expenses, and entry, to one of them. I was born, baptised and confirmed in the Episcopal Church. They have plenty of Homes for elderly persons. I would like to go back to N. Y. and be nearer to where you are—partly because we could meet occasionally, and partly because I like the East. I can find a position in N. Y. that will be as good as the one I have here. I could—and would—keep the one that I have here if it were worth keeping.

It is not my intention to be a mill-stone about your necks, and to weigh you down. There is no reason why I should be. I am not decrepit by any means. There is always work to do, and I must see to it that I do not continue to work like a steam engine and wear myself out, for there's neither sense nor reason in doing it. I am not now working to support a child (nor a scoundrel). I do not need to "make a name," or "grow up" with a business house. I am merely working my way along for a few years until I can enter a "Home" and in the meantime save money to cover it. I have enough money to carry me back to N. Y. and keep me until I find employment.

Do not reply at once. You are both busy now, I know, with the Easter work. Let the matter lie over for a while. Think of it, and speak of it, once in a while. It means responsibility, of course—I would always have to be in touch with you and carry your name in my purse.

Don't do it unless you *really want to.* I won't be vexed if you say no. I respect persons who are sincere. I want you, of course, because I am fond of you both—you are the decentest persons I know—and I am lonely—and alone—and I do need you.

Let me hear from you separately.

Jenny G. Masterson

[To this request that they serve as her "executors" Glenn and Isabel gave an affirmative reply, and invited Jenny to pay them a visit on her way to New York City.]

Chicago, Ill. 4/27/26

Dearest Isabel:

Moving is "some" job, even from one room. Every nail on my left hand is black and blue where I banged on them with the hammer when nailing on the tops. I ache all over. Am not feeling well—my heart aches in every sense of the word—and I am most unnaturally tired. If it is not convenient to meet me on the arrival of our train, don't worry. I shall get a cup of coffee at the Depot "bar" and wait for you in the Waiting Room. Don't rush, or let me put you out too terribly—I love to just loaf, and sit around—I'm dead tired.

The prospect of the trip is full of pleasure to me. I look forward to a delightful weekend with dear Glenn and you. I know Glenn, of course, have known him for a long time. Of course I know you *must* be a nice girl, or Glenn would not have chosen you, but I want to know you, myself—so that even apart from Glenn altogether, you and I can be friends. I hope and pray most earnestly that we may be friends—I need you.

J. G. Masterson

Chicago, Ill. 4/27/26

My dear Glenn:

I enclose a check for fifty ($50) dollars, payable to you. If anything happens to me on my trip East please cash the cheque, and use it for my cremation. If I arrive OK you can let me have the money then.

In case of accident, or death, insist on getting my heavy coat—I shall wear it on the trip East. Sewed in the lining of the coat at bottom hem, left side, is fifty dollars. Five tens. Keep it. I shall have 8 or 10 in my purse, and a $10 bill in a pocket sewed on my corset.

My trunk is with the Am'n Express Co. New York. Claim it and do as you want with it. Mr. Masterson's photographs, and those of Ross, are in the trunk—give them to Ross if you think best, but do not give him anything belonging to me.

My best and dearest love to you.

Jenny G. Masterson

When I get to N. Y. I shall make a proper legal arrangement.

New York City, 6/2/26

My dearest:

. . . We were in Chicago, Ross about 14, one night about midnight I wakened with a start to find the child in his pajamas standing at my bed. I was up in a moment, was he ill? He said "Mother, it's raining"—Yes; was it coming in on his bed? Oh No, he said, but—"Will you come down and see Michigan Avenue in the rain—a lovely, misty, London rain"—We had been gloating over Hopkinson Smiths etchings of London in the rain.

Well, we went. About 8 m'ls down. And it was lovely— And lo! around the corner jogged a hansom cab and *horse,* one of those where the driver sits up high at the back, and Ross and I just cried for joy. We were wet, of course, but it was great. Ross will not forget that night—he will think of it many times. Just as I do, and that will be his punishment. His food and clothes are bought at a high price.

My trip to you is still a delight to me. I can see every tree, and flower—it was lovely. My trip to you was most fortunate—surely the gods urged me to go. I have not been like the same person since, all the "all-gone" lonely, desolate, feeling has left me. I now feel that I "belong"—have a family, and am never alone.

Several days since coming here I have been alone, and never spoke one word, but I can sit in the Park and see your charming little nest, and see you set a delightful meal (I haven't eaten one since) without a bit of fuss, and Glenn everything that is thoughtful and kind, and I think "The Gods are good."

I can see you standing there at the rail as my Boat went out—another couple would have gone away soon as the gangplank was drawn up, but not Glenn and you, and then you became a mere speck, but I didn't feel a bit lonely, for I took you along.

Best love,

Jenny

New York City. Aug. 27/26

My Dearest:

This has been a wonderful week—Prest. Eliot gone—Valentino gone, and the arrival of the Re-incarnation.

One hardly knows whether to laugh at Mrs. Besant, or to feel sorry for her—she has remained on the stage too long. I heard her lecture, in Canada, many years ago, when she first took up with Madame Blavatsky, and after her little doings with Bradlaugh. She was then a very beautiful woman, and a wonderful speaker.

Well, it was a wonderful week for me too. You know, I made a "swear," as Mrs. Katzenjammer says, to accomplish something in the "job" line during August. Maybee I'll write a book some day. The world is funny. I was out every day, rain or shine—mostly rain, and I answered ads by the dozen. Nothing doing. When I got around to Macy's the application form which they handed me to fill out was number *104*. There were 103 applicants ahead of me, and there were so many in the room that there were no empty seats. I was there, standing and sitting, from 10:30 am to 4 pm. Then my no. was called, and I went in. The lady told me right off the bat, that she could not do anything for me. She said "Your education is against you Madam" —Mon Dieu!

I went to Cushman's the big bakery people. Same there—they may take me on to sell bread, after Labor Day. When I went to their Book-Kpg. Dept. the big ignorant boob in charge said they might need help later on in the *Bread Season*. I stammered that I didn't know there was any season for eating bread—I thought people ate bread all the year around. You should see the look he gave me—it said plainly "You poor ignorant simp"—it seems that the sales in bread are only half in summer what they are in winter.

However, all is not lost. I can go down to Brighton and return for 10 cents, and I go. Brighton is 1½ miles beyond Coney, so I go to Brighton (subway) 1 hour, and walk to Coney—1½ mls at the Sea, on our wonderful Boardwalk, or down on the beach—and all for 10 cents. So I go on wet days when I have it all to myself, and I struggle to find my bearings.

Funny, is it not? Clearly I am out of the running, and yet I do not feel old; but probably Mrs. Besant does not feel old either, and Valentino had to step down and out and he was not old.

J. G. M.

N. Y. C. Sept. 2/26

My dearest:

I hope to be among the first to wish you happiness in your new home.

Such a lot of things have happened since you, Glenn dear, and Ross stood in the college office waiting to write on your exam. Tall, thin, pale boys, the world and life all before you—anxious, tense—a long time ago.

If anyone had said then the day would come when you, Glenn dear, the pale, slim boy, would be the only protection of the other boy's mother, you would have been considerably surprised. And then meeting Isabel, and knowing Isabel, and your marriage, and your sweet little nest—it is all wonderful.

The last time I wrote I knew there was something special I wanted to say to you, Isabel dear, but could not, for the life of me, recall what it was, so I just babbled away about something else.

It's your hair. I really think you ought to bob your hair. For one thing almost everyone, old and young, is bobbed now, and one looks peculiar with long hair; and another thing is it is less trouble. Of course Mary Pickford is not bobbed, but pretty near everyone else is.

Best love.

J. G. M.

New York City   Sunday 10/17

My dear Isabel:

So you have passed another mile-stone and the years are slipping by! It does not seem so long ago since I sent you a greeting from Chicago, but many things have happened since then.

I feel sure you have made your house into a home, but wish you could have found a small apartment, for I suppose a house means keeping up the fire, and the hot water, which must be a nuisance.

Thank you so much for remembering me when making your pilgrimage. Graves Hall has a very warm spot in my heart—I shall go there again, and sit on that bench facing the canal. It was in Graves Hall where Ross and Glenn were friends—after Ross left Graves Hall he fell entirely under the spell of his "Belovéd Mother"—his "B-M"—the old Smythe woman —or is she a woman? After that time he was nothing at all to me —or rather I was nothing at all to him—he had found "another Mother."

Well, my dear, I have had a "job" since writing you—in fact *two* of them. I am still in the second one.

In August I was a very sick lady—ate little, and slept less. It was a common experience to waken up at 2 am. Oh! so wide awake! lie in agony of mind till 3, get up and read until 5, etc. etc. So I took the first job I could get—it was in a Dept. store—I was not selling—I was a "floor woman"—on my feet all day long—horrible crowd—a basement—I suffered death. At night I was "all in," aching from head to toe, and on the 4th day in my "job" I fainted at noon. I came "home" in a cab, and never went back. It was of no use trying—I would rather be dead. I was in bed for a week and in that time I decided to go "home," see my tree in the Don Valley—"Notre Pont" where Mr. M. and I carved our initials on the railing, try my luck in my own country, and if I fail, end it there (maybe). I wrote to one of my sisters—she is a widow living with her son in Montreal. She replied at once, and invited me home for a rest. She thinks I intend to return to N. Y. but I don't, not if I can help it, but I shall not impose on her too terribly long, so let her think anything she wants to.

Well, my finances were running low. I had only planned on having enough to carry me along until October hence the second job. My work is similar to the other job, and is very heavy, but I can stand it for another week. That is what has kept me going—counting every day, hour even, until it ends. I sat here like a miser every night counting my money—it is almost funny; I "dine" at the Automat, do my own laundry evenings, am pains and aches from head to toe, but I think "if I can only drag along 2 weeks more—one week—etc." and now the time has passed, and I shall leave my "job" on next Saturday. I shall put my things in storage, and take chances about coming back. Even if I have to come back, I shall never again try to find office employment in N. Y. I shall try schools—Institutions—Hotels—Clubs, and by making this trip home it will decide in my mind definitely whether I can, or can not, live among my own people, and in my own country.

I shall know about the excursion next week, and will let you know about it; if no excursion, I have planned to leave N. Y. on October 30, Saturday, reaching home on Sunday. My best love to both.

Jenny

New York City, 10/26–26

My dear Isabel:

That was a lovely surprise—I was delighted. Indeed Marco Polo will be a joy to me on the trip—needless to say that I shall not take a berth, and as most of the trip will be at night Marco will be a charming companion. Indeed I have been tempted several times in the last few days to take a peep into the book, but am glad to say that I put Satan behind me, and am keeping our friend Donn for the train.

When in Montreal I intend to attend at least one service in "All Saints" where I was confirmed by the Bishop of Toronto; I wore a piece of point lace on my head, so the dear man would not have to touch my hair with his hand—and I trembled a great deal, and prayed to be "good." That's a long time ago. I always took everything so seriously, and it is a great mistake—spoiled my whole life. I did not know then that Life was just a farce—a joke. I thought it was a serious thing, and worth living.

There is something pathetic, after all these years, about going back "home" to see a *tree*.

J. G. M.

New York City   *Oct. 20/26*

My dearest and best:

In another hour I shall be on my way, and watching the lights of N. Y. grow less and less, but I want to say a word to you before leaving. I have taken your name from my purse—there *may* be a wreck, you know, and it would not be fair to carry your name. All the money I have is on my person, sewn in my coat, my corset, etc. It will cover my expenses if the call comes before I reach home, and Grace (my sister) is, of course, the person to claim me.

I just had to go, Glenn dear—life in my 5th story room, with my heartaches was unbearable. It may be that I shall remain in Montreal, but if I cannot remain—and I would like to, it will not break my heart to come back. New York, in my opinion, stands alone.

Address me "General Delivery, Montreal, Canada." I want my sister to understand that I am only a transient.

You have been a great help and comfort to me—I want Isabel and you to remember that.

Jenny

Montreal, Canada   *12/15/26*

My dearest and best:

On tomorrow, or the next day, I shall answer in detail your kind and thoughtful letter. My visit to Montreal has, and has not, been a success; for what I gained in one way I have lost in another. It has, however, helped to clear up the mental haze in which I was enveloped while in New York, and when I return to New York, as I plan to do very soon, I shall, at last, know where I stand. No more longing to see "my own"— no more hankering after the tree in the Don Valley, or the beaten track down the Rosedale Ravine. All of that sort of stuff will be wiped off the slate, and I may possibly become a practical and useful person.

My visit to my sister Grace only covered a couple of weeks; she is quite a sick woman, suffers from diabetes, and is not in any way placed to have a guest; so I rented this one-room apartment—quite a lovely place, and started out "on my own" to hunt a "job." The Christmas season is not a good time to select for such a quest. Everyone is too concerned about their own personal affairs to pay any attention to a wanderer. So, the upshot of the whole thing is, that I have just decided to make another flitting. (I am "some" flitter, dear Glenn.) Circumstances are such that I do not want to spend Christmas in Montreal. I shall go to the automat in N. Y. as I have gone so many times, and while it will not be a "merry" Christmas, it will be better than being here, and I shall not be unhappy.

Ask dear Isabel *not* to send any Christmas gift this year, but to send a note so I may receive it about Christmas time, in N. Y. and so not feel so desperately alone.

You have my best love, and deep gratitude—my crimes cannot have been so terrible when I can win, and hold, the affection of such persons as Isabel and you. You have been, and are, a great comfort to me.

Jenny

Montreal, Canada. Dec. 17/26

My dearest Boy and Girl:

. . . Grace never was a housekeeper, and just drifts along in any old way. She used to be a great reader when she was young, but now she regrets having "wasted" so much time on books. She suffers from diabetes, but it would be silly to pity 'her as she has a good time—eats what she fancies, sleeps when she pleases—lets the house go to thunder—and lives along from day to day in any sort of way. She has enough money to keep her, and her youngest son (22) lives with her. My other sisters are entirely the reverse; they are entirely up-to-date and refined. Their homes are lovely. But, alas! the thinking members of the family do not want me—they could never, never, believe in divorce. As a result, I am tolerated—received kindly, etc. but *not* one of the family. There are subjects that must always be a closed book between us. After the first pleasure of meeting them was over, I felt more lonely when with them than I have ever been without them.

I am going back to mad Bedlam—New York and the Automat. It is quite a pitiful state of affairs, but what can one do? Nothing can alter the fact that I ran away with a divorced man when there wasn't even a divorce court in England (or Canada) and that we lived in the U. S. the criminal dumping ground of the world. The stain could never be washed off—I carry the Scarlet Letter.

I can now live alone, if I have to, but I do not have to, for I have Isabel and you. I can *never* have been a wicked person, or Isabel and you would have sensed it and rejected me. My spirits are fine—in better shape now than they have experienced in years. Where will I spend Christmas? In New York. I shall attend service in the Little Church Around the Corner, and thank the God Who knows and understands all our motives, and all our thoughts, that I am *not* alone, but have found "abiding love" in Isabel and you.

Always,

Jenny

Montreal, Canada   *12/20/26*

My dearest Glenn:

. . . You name is again in my bag in its old place, and I hope soon to have more money in order to protect you from money loss in case of accident to me.

Should you have to pay out money to cover me, please try to locate Ross and allow him to re-imburse you. I have enough money in a pocket in my corset and in my handbag to cover my expenses in N. Y. for two weeks. My goods are with the Gray Storage Co. 9th Avenue, N. Y. Claim them.

Oh, yes, my Christmas will be happy—I have Isabel and you.

Best love,

Jenny G. Masterson

> *General Delivery*
> *New York City*
> *Jan. 5/27*

My dearest Isabel:

Sometimes I feel ashamed for not writing to you, and then I think it best to wait until tomorrow and maybe that day's mail would bring me something definite in the way of employment, and so tomorrow comes, and still tomorrow, and nothing definite. Hunting a "job" is not a pleasant occupation when one is past 30.

Your Christmas letter and your Christmas box were wonderful. One could never be quite forsaken or alone when one receives such things on Christmas Eve. I appreciate them greatly.

The Princeton sheet was a great treat. I love Princeton. It was the seat of my hopes and dreams for many years and a great part of me is buried there.

The "envelope" covered both dinners—thanks to you—Christmas and New Year. I don't know how my money lasts so long, it's almost uncanny, but I suppose it's because I never waste a cent—never "blow in" a penny—your coat saved me the price of a coat, for I needed one, so I saved that money, and your "envelope" covered several dinners, and so stretches out my diminishing funds. It was very thoughtful of you.

My Irish cup with the Japanese design is lovely—first evening I spend in my "own place" I shall make some of your tea, and use the green cup—it will seem like having company. I shall also burn the incense on that same evening. Tonight I had a splendid bath, and used my new soap—it's delightful—soothing and splendid. One doesn't have to wait for "Saturday night" here, for a bath, there is a wonderful supply of hot water all the time. My green wash cloth is on the dresser, folded into a diamond shape, and used as a mat. It's very nice.

I can quite appreciate what you say, Isabel dear, regarding my trip to Canada, and my inability to "fit in" or feel happy there; but the circumstances in connection with my life, all the way through, have been unusual, and are not easily understood. Suppose that Ross knew that I am just about on my last $50, don't you believe he would send me money? I do. Well, why? Would it be because he loves me? Oh, no. If Ross loved me, or even had a sentimental regard for me because of my relation to him, he would never have given his money, his time, and thoughts to a common sporting woman while I worked 12 hours a day, and was so ill—so dreadfully ill—no fire in my room —no window—no blanket on my bed—no winter coat. No, my dear, that's not love, or if it is, I don't want it. Yet Ross would send me money. Why? Well, it would be an easy way to buy ease for his own conscience—to keep me quiet—to cover an obligation. That's all.

It's much the same way with my people at home. My Father dropped dead one day, and had no provision made for his family—7 of them, all under 18. Not one in the house capable of earning a penny. It was my salary that kept the house going. I happened to work myself into a good paying position when yet quite young, and it all went to the house. No one ever denied it, or pretended to think otherwise, and when I dared to marry the man I had been in love with for years, but dreaded to take my money out of their house (I never did do it until they were all provided for) why, they said I was like the cow that gave the milk and then kicked the pail.

That was because Mr. Masterson was a divorced man, and that consequently I was "ruined" and a disgrace to the family. Yes, my people would give me things to eat—sure they would, but not because they love me. It would be just the same as Ross. It's a strange story—I can't for the life of me see *why* I have been so cursed—what did I do?

My best love to both. A Happy New Year.

Jenny

New York City   Jan. 9/27

My dearest Boy:

Altho' I haven't anything very definite to tell in this letter, yet I've taken some steps ahead, for I am now *working a plan.* You know, the Christmas week was just no time at all to go out hunting a job, so I didn't go. The weather—when it wasn't raining—was perfectly splendid, and I tramped thro' Central Park—and tramped down to City Hall for my mail, and read some, and thought a lot. This is my plan:—I want, if possible, to get employment by the day, in order to keep my own room and be able to shut out the world every evening. But considering the fact that my money is getting low (altho' I'm not yet on the last 50) and that *I* am not getting any younger, and *should* have a little nest-egg laid by, I determined not to accept a very low salary—not to look for that sort of position—and unless I can find a permanent position paying, at least, 20 to start, to give up the idea of keeping my own room, and seek indoor employment. So I wrote to some men I know and asked for employment. I received the replies, but there was no encouragement in them. No one wants to re-employ a woman of my age. Then I wrote to the Clubs—Harvard—Yale—Dartmouth—to the Housekeepers, asking for any sort of household work in the club. If one of them offers me anything I shall accept it. You see, I am not trained in any household work—it's a question if they would take me as a chambermaid even, but short of scrubbing, or cooking, I would be glad to get in. I shall wait for 3 or 4 days, and then I shall go around to the big hotels, the Plaza—Astor—Commodore, etc. and try to get in as something. Maybe as the hall woman—don't know what her title is, but she sits in the hallway (an ofc) and takes the keys, and I think keeps an eye on things generally—the Linen Room—or chamber work. Whatever I can get. In the meantime I am answering ads for companion—housekeeper—etc.

I'd hate like everything to have a *mistress*, but there are motherless homes, and in that case (if they don't want me to *wash*) I would be good to the kids—if there's not too many of them.

It would be a trouble—and a bit of a heartache—to have to share a room with some of the "other servants"; but one has to get used to things, and if I can save money it would not have to last for always. You remember our friend Swinburne. "I thank with deep thanksgiving Whatever Gods may be, That no man lives for ever—That dead men rise up never— And even the weariest river Flows, somewhere, safe to Sea."

Something is bound to turn up, and Mister Micawber has nothing on me.

Oh! Let me tell you something that occurred before I left for Canada, in Oct. I had intended to remain in Canada if I could, but to decide definitely whether I could, or not, and I rather hungered to hear something of Ross before leaving the country, perhaps for good.

I went to see the minister who performed the ceremony. It was a funny little place—seems as tho' the church (Baptist) and the minister's house are under the same roof. A poor place. The minister is old—indifferent—sleepy. He said he did not know the pair at all—had never seen, or heard of either of them before they presented a license, paid the fee, had no friends with them—just the 2 of them—and the minister's wife stood up as witness. He has never heard of them since—knows nothing at all about them. He yawned a good deal, and was evidently rather bored. Isn't that a queer thing? The girl was born in the place, and owns property there—I saw it—and her mother's brother, a Dr. lives next door, quite prominent people, all of them wealthy. Why select this stupid old man, and be married in his parlor without a single friend present. What do you make of that.

My best love to both.

J.

My dearest Girl:

My luck! My luck in quest of a job is something to be either laughed about, or wept about. I am trying to do the laughing. It's hardly possible that anyone in N.Y. works harder than I. I am out every day, rain or shine (it's mostly rain) from early until late—tramped a blister on my heel—tramped a hole in the sole of my shoe, and in the heel of my rubber. I gaze at them in dismay for it means wet feet, and wet feet are the first step toward pneumonia, and, to be honest, I'm beginning to be scared.

I've been just about everywhere—sometimes full of hope, and then in the Slough of Despond. An agency sent me to a children's Home, they wanted a night watch for the Babies. I'm not hankering after night work, but would have taken it. It took an hour in the sub. to get to it, and then lo! they must have a graduated nurse!

Then the agencies send me to faraway places and when I get there the Matron or Supt. has already made a selection, and in this way I often lose half a day. Another Home thought I did not look strong enough to work with children—and they nearly all want trained workers, or professional nurses. It is the same with the Social Svc. people.

I met kind people, but—the hole is still in my shoe, and my toes flop up and down in the wet. However, I'm not grumbling—not kicking—not wholly discouraged, *yet*. There must be a turn in the Lane somewhere, and I have not tried the Hotels yet. I certainly do dread having to go into a private house as "general" and anyway I simply don't know how to cook—and a "mistress" would be a horror.

More later—and I hope better and brighter news. *Don't slip away* from me—keep close.

Jenny

"*Home*"   *Thursday, Jan.* 27

My dearest and best:

The Money Order reached me yesterday evening—what can I say? An ordinary "Thank you" means so little, or so much, that it does not express my feelings at all. But you understand, I feel sure. You can appreciate the position I am in, and the jump my heart gave when I opened your letter, and saw your very substantial sign of friendship and sympathy. You know—everyone knows—that to touch one's pocket book is a sure test of friendship. The "friend in need" etc. It is so easy to have "friends" when it costs nothing. And what a wonderful sifting out, and test this experience of a few years has been to me. You are just splendid.

I shall do exactly as you say and keep this order until after I draw my first salary. If they keep me here to commence a second month, my position is practically secure, and I shall then return the money to you; but if they do not retain my services here, then I shall keep your loan for a longer time, and have it to use when again on the hunt for a "job." I had to invest in a few things before coming here, and that made heavy inroads on my 50. My shoes ½ soled and heels, Hosiery, N'gowns, etc., and *glasses*. The glasses are a heavy bill as they must be bifocal, but I simply had to get them, my sight was so very poor, and anyway, they were nose glasses, and one can't wear those when bobbing up and down attending small children. Then the agency has charged $11.50 for sending me here—it's pretty steep. But it's all right. Everything is all right if I can only remain here for, at least, 6 mos. I can save enough in that time to meet an emergency.

J. G. M.

Feb. 10/27

[Written across the top of this letter: Please use a seal when you reply, or use 2 envelopes, writing across the flap of the inside one. They may open my letters. J.]

My dearest:

. . . My dear, if you ever have a child and are so unhappy as not to be in a position to personally take care of it, I beg you *never* to place it in such an Inst'n as this; if there is no other course open to you, then take the child to the sea and shove him in. I was never at any time tempted to place Ross in any sort of Institution, and oh! how I thank my stars for saving me.

I would rather be dead than remain in this place. I am just only a whipper, a common spanker of little children, a beast, a cur, for $50 a month. The children are as young as 3 years—think of it! *3 years.* There's a little fellow of 3, pink all over, and bright sunny hair like a sunbeam. I told him (when I came first—*now* I'm just a beast) that he was my Sunbeam, and that brought him more than one spanking and pretty near cost me my $50. God! how I despise myself for accepting money for spanking babies. There's a tiny child, white all over, her hair cream, her little body pure white, I called her my Snow flower, and that was pretty near being my Waterloo.

It's too shameful for words—for the first time in my life I despise myself thoroughly, and am ashamed. For 10 days my lips throbbed with fever, and had great slits in them— I was in a bad mental and physical condition, and still am. My heart literally trembles *all* the time—its palpitation is terrible, and to lie on my left side is quite impossible. Then I formed my decision, and now I feel a little better, altho' of course, a cur, but every day brings me nearer to the end. I refuse to stay here. Soon as I have money enough to warrant my leaving, I shall certainly do so.

The conditions are a trifle unusual, I think. The nice lady I met on coming here first is the Matron, and we seldom see each other. I have nothing at all to do with the Matron. I am in the Nursery Dept. There is a Supervisor, a 1st Asst. and 2nd Asst. I am the latter. That means 2 bosses. The Supervisor is practically new—only here 2 mos. The 1st Asst. has been here a couple of years, so you see that the Supervisor is very much dependent on her. She is a Devil if ever there was one; she has a little thin squeaky voice, a sort of whine, and thin cruel lips. She dislikes me, has from the first moment. In the first 10 days it was common to hear one of those women (Beasts) say as they spanked the babies, "Now Just see Mrs. Masterson squirm" —and sure enough, she did squirm, all the blood in her body rushed to her head, and she wanted to go screaming mad. The children are not marked—haven't a scar on them—it is all done on the legs, their little bumty-bum, and arms. They are taught simply nothing at all by us—except to hate humanity. Not a story —not a game—They go to Kindergarten morning and afternoon, and I believe they are happy there, but we see only to their physical needs. We bathe them *twice* a week—mend clothing (think of the pile of darning) polish their shoes every morning— spank them to bed—spank them out of bed—never a kind word. Terrible. Our hours are very long. I often work from 5:30 to 9 or 9:30. The short rest in the afternoon amounts to nothing—I'm afraid to sleep, for fear of not wakening in time, but I fall into a stupid doze the moment I sit down.

Well, I'll write again—I've been too terribly fatigued to write lately; was scared to death I was going to be ill, but now that I've made up my mind what to do, I feel better.

It's a shameful thing to accept money for spanking little children—their little faces will haunt me as long as I live.

You have my best love—must go to bed— I am utterly worn out—but there are many things I want to say to you.

Jenny

Hell. Sunday, Feb. 20/27

My Dearest:

There are many things I want to say, but first let me thank you both most earnestly for standing so close to me during the past month, one of the most trying and horrible experiences of my entire life.

I am glad dear Glenn used a seal on his last letter; Friend No. 1 handed the letter to me in the Nursery, turned it over and looked at the seal, then said "open it." I merely took the letter, said "Thank you," and opening my dress slipped it into my bosom. She glared at me and said "You can open and read it." I replied "I know I can." You should have seen her face. I never said a word.

We have a thin child whose back bone is sharp, he wets the bed. The way they beat that child is a crime. One day he sat *all day* with his face to the wall—not a word, not a toy, all day. Today he sat on the floor, in the dormitory, alone, face to the wall, all morning.

Oh, you should see little Eddie—the darling, lovely boy of 3. Soon as those Devils find out that I particularly love one child they make a point of beating him. One evening he came to me and held up his beautiful little face, he said "I can't *always* be a good boy because I am only a *little* boy." Can it be possible that a *God*—all powerful—would allow those frightful things to happen.

My little Sun-beam boy is not allowed to speak to me—I cannot even bathe him—and he did so love to be a "fish" in the tub. You should see the woe-begone looks he gives me; he, too, is 3.

"Mrs. Masterson (strong emphasis on the Mrs.) will you please remember that you are in an Institution, and *not* receiving $100 a month for giving individual attention to the children"—I hear that every day.

But yesterday! Saturday—that was the straw that broke the camel's back. There is no school on Saturday, and that means the Nursery *all day* for the children. After breakfast we polished the shoes—40 pair—the children were ordered to sit still and not speak or move. The noise was not great, but Devil No. 1 got mad and ordered them all to stand, close their eyes, and place their hands on the top of their heads.

As sure as there is a God in Heaven (if there be) they stood that way for *one hour and 20 minutes.*

I could have screamed. (I was mending.) If the children moved they got whacked across the legs, and then got whacked to stop crying. (Remember the babies of 3—1 hour and 20 minutes.) Finally they were ordered to sit down, but *not a word.* They sat down and here and there we heard baby talking, and then to my unspeakable horror I saw that infernal Devil (my Boss) get a big sheet of sticking plaster—cut it into strips—and *paste the babies lips together.* It was put on star-wise. I nearly went mad. You should see the expression of those children's eyes. There they sat, all pasted up. No, the Devils did not ask me to do it—they did it all. But when dinner-time came, we couldn't get the plaster off. I don't know how those Fiends managed it, but when I came to wash them, the marks *would* not come off with soap and water. I think those Hell-hounds were scared, for they whispered together and kept looking at me. I saw myself in a glass and I looked like a dead woman.

At 3 o'clock, when off for an hour, I went straight to my room, and wrote my resignation, and placed it on the matron's desk.

Now I feel better. Will leave on March 1. Do *not* send any more mail to this God-forsaken hole.

J. G. M.

Feb. 22, 1927

My Dearest:

My last told of the Saturday's doings where the Devils plastered up the dear helpless children, and of my rushing away to resign. My resignation read: "I beg to resign my position in the Home for Foundlings. Will you kindly let me know if it will be convenient to you to release me on March 1, or sooner?" You see I make no explanation, no accusations. That evening the Matron sat beside me while I waited for the children —they had not finished supper. She was very kind, asked the "why" etc. I told her a thing or two.

Sunday passed as usual—same spankings.

On Monday morning our numerous instruments of torture had disappeared, and we hadn't a thing to beat the babies with. Storm was plainly stamped on the faces of the Devils—neither of them said good morning to me, or addressed me in any way. The children were entirely beyond control, and terribly noisy! The little squeaky voice of Devil No. 2 simply wasn't heard. At 3 o'clock the children came up from school, all jumping and shouting. Devil No. 1 ordered toys to be given them—kiddie cars—drums—dolls, etc. They seldom or never get the toys because they made a noise with them, but on Monday they were all there. I was amazed. Then Devil No. 1 turned to me with a flaming face, and she certainly gave me one good setting out; it seems they had told her of my resignation, and why, and she was surely a mad lady. She screamed that she would now teach me a thing or two, and show the House how *I* could govern the children without spanking them. Well, my dears, I may be a fool, but I'm not such a fool as to be caught in such a fool-trap as that.

I hadn't said a word, but now I spoke. I told the lady that the only one thing she could by any chance teach me was to despise such beasts as she, in women's clothing. I reminded her that she had ruined the children by teaching them that the whip was the only form of correction to be heeded, and that it would take months to undo her vile and barbarous teaching. I said that if she dreamed for one moment that I was subservient to her in any way she was making the mistake of her life; that she could not *make* me do anything or make me fall into any fool-traps she might set, for I refused to remain in any room with her for even 10 minutes; and as a proof of that I walked out and closed the door. You should have seen their faces—they were frozen dumb.

I went straight downstairs and told the Matron; she said that of course it was a trick and that when I failed to govern the children, the Devils would have had the Supt. come up to see the mess I was in. She requested me to go back and remain until the 1st, and that they would discharge Devil No. 1, but I said that I would never again stand in the Nursery. So that was final.

She fell all over herself to be nice to me. I think they are afraid of me, that I may force a public investigation, or something of that kind—they clearly want to be friendly with me.

More later.

J.

Feb. 25/27

My Dears:

You have no idea what a popular lady your humble servant has become—quite a social lion. It's good as a play. 5 women visited my room in one evening to congratulate, and thank me, for speaking up on behalf of the children. 2 women who work here as servants and whose children are in the house have come to shake hands with me. I work in the sewing room mending the children's clothes—hours 9 to 5. Twice the Matron has come to enquire if I am "greatly fatigued" and if so, to go to my room and rest for an hour.

But my head is not swollen. I can see thro' the little play without any trouble at all.

The only letter from you that has reached me in this house (I mean the *last* letter) is the one bearing a seal. Do not write here again. I shall leave on Monday.

My best love to both.

New York City   Wednesday

My Dears:

Well, it's over now, and it certainly was a stormy trip; everything ends—sometime. For 2 nights, now, I've been dead to the world for 12 solid hours—utterly worn out. As Mrs. Katzenjammer says "Too much is enough."

I am a sick lady. I who could tramp all over N.Y. am tired to death when I crawl along 20 blocks or so. I must get myself into better shape.

My next will be of other things—the curtain has fallen on all "Institute" life for me. I must form other plans.

My best love to both.

J.

Sunday. 3/27

My dear Isabel:

I haven't written much lately, because I wanted to give you a rest—and I dread wearing out my welcome. Sometimes friends become a burden. My quest for a "job" is sometimes comic, but is generally tragic—my star of hope has not yet set, but it's getting low.

Jenny

Wednesday   3/25/27

My dearest and best:

Surely Monday was my lucky day—I heard from you, and found a position. Do not write until you hear from me again—am on my step out to the "job"—it is here in the City—a resident position.

Thank you so much for your lovely letter—I wish you were indeed my son. More later.

Jenny

New York City—Tuesday May 3/27

My dearest and best:

My position here in the Hospital is certainly strenuous, to say the least; we have 100 maids and porters, and the building covers a block. I walk a thousand miles a day, and as for steps! I dream of them.

My feet gave out—became greatly swollen and painful, and I limp. I now wear bandages, and that helps some, but the floors are all tile, and the steps white marble (I'm strong on marble steps and pillars, you see) and many of our women, nurses and maids, either limp or wear high laced shoes. I am assistant Housekeeper.

Ross's letter to you does not surprise me —it was, as you say, merely a feeler, and you will hear from him again. You are free to say anything you desire to him. What you say is sure to be the wise, and best, thing. You are such a good friend to me that I trust you implicitly—your good judgment, and your kindness. I have felt for a long time that he is not living with the woman, but the fact that he sold his mother for a meal ticket still remains. Do, and say, whatever you think is best.

I am very tired, and ache; cannot write much tonight, but next Thursday pm is my "day" off duty, and I shall spend it writing to you—I have many things to tell you. More later.

Jenny

New York City   5/5/27

My dearest Boy:

My heart and my mind are full of my visit to Mr. Pratt this afternoon, and I must speak of that first. He has had a visit from Ross. Ross has evidently impressed Mr. Pratt so strongly with his being a model son, and that I am, and was, merely a bad-tempered, disagreeable, "jealous" person, that Mr. Pratt believes it. You know, Glenn dear, that if I had wanted to find Ross, I could have done so at any time within a few hours, and the reason I did not find him is because I did not wish to. The idea of my holding out the olive branch to Ross at this time, he living in New York and never having made the smallest effort to learn anything about me, is too disgusting for words.

Speaking about money reminds me of the 25 you sent. Mr. Pratt still has the money. If he has a check acct. I shall ask him to keep the 25 and send you a check for that amount. If not I shall send you a draft next week.

You are my great standby—my only hope. Tell Isabel that you and she must never believe that I am, or ever was, just a crazy "jealous" fool, and that Ross is a martyr. More later.

Jenny

New York City   *June 13/27*

My dearest Boy:

Thank you so much for the card—it was lovely of you to send it, for I know you are swamped in work between exams and the move.

I would have written to you long ago, but I, too, am swamped in work. It has been a question with me whether I can stand it, and indeed it is still a question. The work is very constant, and very heavy—Sunday and Monday, all alike, from 6 am until any hour in the evening, often 9 or 10 o'clock. Unforeseen things are always happening in a hospital, and to keep regular hours is not possible. In many respects the place suits me, and I suit it. I still love my snow white gown and our marble halls, and Mrs. Graham, the Housekeeper, and I act as one person, but my heart gives out, and I find difficulty in breathing—cannot lie on my left side, and that sort of thing, and so that's the way.

I started a bank account last month; will send you the particulars in my next, and will try to make some definite plans regarding my affairs. A lady with a bank acct. and heart disease, should make a will.

All my love as of yore.

Jenny

Telegram received by Isabel and Glenn when Jenny heard of the birth of their son Donald:

MAY THE GODS ALWAYS BE GOOD TO LITTLE
DONALD AND TO HIS DEAR PARENTS.
JENNY MASTERSON

Sunday   *Aug. 7/27*

My dearest Girl:

It is not a very nice day here, dark and threatening rain, very damp—but it would be a glorious day, despite the weather, if I might drop into your garden and kiss the toes of sweet Donald, under the tree. You are a sensible mother, I feel sure, and do not keep the dear Baby too terribly muffled up and warm—I often feel sorry for babies, they are so terribly wrapped in blankets and clankets. And then you won't feed him to death, or allow well-meaning friends to joggle him up and down, or kiss his dear face. He is, indeed, a fortunate young man. When you write please tell me where you got his name, and why.

I am again on the "Shanghraun." No, you won't find that word in an English dictionary. It's Irish, and it means on the "go," or marching along, tramping.

It was only after I had slept *15* hours a day for 3 days that I began to realize how desperately tired, and shaky, I am. I could not sit down anywhere without falling asleep; it's a wonder I haven't lost my purse for it has, more than once, slipped from my arm to my feet.

My great jump in salary from $60 per to 120 per only lasted 2 weeks, yet it helps along, and is welcome, and needed. I must rest—am tired to death. Ten servants walked out with me, in protest. We left the work badly crippled.

You see, Mrs. Graham, the housekeeper, was a great favorite with the help. Her brother in Augusta, Me. died suddenly. She went to the funeral. I was given to understand that I was holding her position for her, and I worked my fool-head off; was congratulated from every side—the house never so clean—the help all stood together and close to me—everything went along without a hitch. Then suddenly it was announced that the house had written Mrs. Graham *not to come back*. It was very mean—She had been there 1½ years, her things were scattered about, etc. not packed. They appointed a new Housekeeper—a German. Then the fun commenced. From the moment our Kaiser friend entered the door she antagonized everyone she met; she is over-bearing, arrogant, insulting, ignorant. We were all stunned. She treated me as if I were dirt under her feet. I remained one day with her, then left.

Jenny

Aug. 9/27

My dearest Boy:

Now that you have had time to grasp the idea that you are a "Daddy," and the father of a family, I venture to send you a "business" letter; had I sent it a couple of weeks ago you would probably have lost the check, and you know, my dear, you will now need all the checks you can lay your hands on. Having a family is a big responsibility when one possesses a moral sense.

Altho' my exit from the Hospital was very hurried, it cannot be said to have been sudden, for I had figured it out that, from a physical standpoint, I could not remain there very long. The work was constant, and very heavy. I was on my feet from 6 am to any time about midnight, and always on the run—in the basement one moment, on the 7th floor the next—a dozen things to see to at one time. My experience was very interesting, for I never dreamed I could "run" such a huge concern, and, let me say, I am *the only housekeeper* in several years who has left that institution *of her own accord*.

When you sent me that $25 I made up my mind not to use it except in extreme necessity. So I had given it to Mr. Pratt to keep in his safe. When one is hungry and has $25 at hand, one is tempted to use it, while they *may* pull thro' without it with an effort. So it remained with Mr. Pratt until our break, and in the meantime I had gone to the Hospital. After that I was literally too busy to even think of the check.

Now, however, I enclose it to you with a thousand thanks, and blessings. I will get along.

Jenny

Aug. 25/27

My dearest Girl:

Mrs. Graham (the Housekeeper) has come back to N.Y. She called me by phone one evening and I was delighted. She lives with her daughter, Mrs. Elliott, away up at the very top of Manhattan—I have spent an evening with them. Mrs. G is hunting another housekeeping job, and I am waiting (for a while) until she gets it, and then she will get me into the same house as "something"—any old thing I can do. That sounds queer, does it not? A crazy, fool-plan? Well, I know.

In the first place a sort of terror seizes me when I think of going into a new job; an unaccountable, but very real *fear*. I've lost my grip. In the next place I am not physically fit—my sight became so bad, in the Hospital, that I could hardly see objects in front of me. My heart literally "quivers"—I feel it quiver. If I attempt hard work and drop dead, it would be fine, but—Would I drop dead? What would happen if I merely became ill, paralysed, or some fool thing?

I have stood on a rock, and on a bridge, but have not the courage to leap off. Am just an ordinary coward.

Everyone, as is anyone, is out of town, anyway. Many of the employment agencies are closed until September. It will soon be September, however, and then I shall wake up, and get busy.

Jenny

Thursday   *Sept. 1*

My dear:

. . . Do you get time to read much? Last week I finished "Elmer Gantry," the most disgusting piece of ignorance, vulgarity, and lies that I have ever run across. How the man ever got anyone to publish it is a mystery to me. In order to house-clean my mind, and get a better taste in my mouth, I am now deep in the history of art—How to study pictures—the pictures of the Louvre—the Vatican—etc.

But I must soon hustle out and get a job. Pray to the weatherman for a few days sun if you have any influence with him.

Jenny

N.Y.C. Sept. 26/27

My dearest Boy:

The picture is lovely—I am delighted to have it; under a magnifying glass the Darling's dear face is quite clear, and is, of course, the "living picture of his Dad."

My life, if it can be called life, is certainly not an ordinary one. I pass days and days in this glorious city and never open my lips to a soul except to ask the grocer for a loaf or a pint of milk. My recent move has not been an improvement, but "all things pass" you know. "Art alone enduring stays to us; The bust out-lives the throne, The coin Tiberius."

I've a prospect of going to a small sanitarium 40 miles north of here. Mrs. Graham is there now. I had a line on a couple of other things but they fell through. However, there is always another day. The more I knew of Mrs. Graham the less I liked her—we are not mates—another god with clay feet.

When you write again please let me know if you have heard anything more from Ross, or if your getting in touch has terminated, and if so in what manner.

My thoughts and best wishes are often with you and your little family. May the Gods continue to smile on you all.

Jenny

Brooklyn, N. Y. Nov. 2/27

My dearest Boy and Girl:

Here I am again—at last; it seemed as tho' I could never again get around to writing a letter, but you have been in my thoughts constantly.

There's a lot to tell—I was desperately alone, and ill. The house on 76th Street had become unbearable, not one single person of even half decent character in the entire apartment; they came in and out all night, mostly drunk, and I was literally afraid of them. To think of *paying* to live with such people was a joke. So I sent a note to Ross and asked him to meet me in the Library; on that same day I found a position in the Linen Room, The University Club.

The result of the whole thing was that I rented a one room apartment in the same building with Ross—he already occupied a one room apt. here, my apartment is next door to his, on the same floor; it seemed to be providential. Our arrangement is quite satisfactory to each of us—we each run our own show; Ross has his own furniture, books, radio, etc—I, my own little treasures. He drops in every evening to say "goodnight." Sometimes it's quite late, and we meet as friends. We have no confidences, no explanations, no promises. I have not asked him one personal question, he lives alone; if he chooses to tell me things later on, all right, if not, it will suit me. I expect nothing, and it is not in his power to disappoint, or hurt me—ever again. "Blessed is he that expecteth nothing for he shall never be disappointed." I expect nothing. He looks very thin, and he has a number of gray hairs; I think he has been through some deep waters. First day I came here I found a little electric stove all ready to make a cup of tea, the tea, sugar, cups, etc. and a beautiful *red rose*. I believe he is glad to have me here, it was entirely his suggestion.

Ross's apt. is larger than mine, he has an open grate, a mantel, and *all* our books. They are entirely separate apartments, but open on the same hall. Ross has his things. I have mine.

My "job" is not a permanent one; the woman whose place I hold met with an accident, fell down a stairway (at home) and broke her arm. When she has recovered she will return, and then I leave. She has been with the Club 10 yrs. so that the position is hers whenever she is ready to claim it.

So you see I am all "sot up" and am happier than I have been in many a long day. Let me say that I have a lease on this apt. so my address is fixed for a year, and I shall do *any sort* of work to keep going as I am now headed.

Jenny

Brooklyn, N. Y. Jan. 7/28

My dearest Boy and Girl:

There is so much for me to tell about that I can never put half of it on paper—wish I might drop in some evening and "talk your heads off" and so catch up on my news. You remember I was with the University Club for 6 or 8 weeks. Then the woman whose place I filled returned to work—she had been with the Club 10 years—and so I was again on the Shanghraun (that's Irish). In the meantime I had moved out here to Brooklyn Heights—a lovely place—and was busy fixing up my apartment. It takes time, and considerable hauling of packing cases to convert them into tables, chiffoniers, etc. I was out of salary, however, only about 10 days when I found another "job." By that time we were close on Thanksgiving and I wanted to be under pay during the holiday season. This time it was in a Dept. store, and again in the place of a girl absent because of sickness. That means temporary work. They placed me in the picture dept. Fate was kind in sending me to the picture dept. The only other person in the dept. (she is buyer and everything) has been there for over 20 years, and she is, without exception, one of the most ignorant women I have ever known. She is a devout Catholic—one of the way-down-low Irish ones—and she knows as much about pictures, or art in any line, as Paddy's pig. She says no one can "learn me nothing about pictures, I know all there is to know." I stared at her in astonishment, and could hardly believe my ears—but there she stood, brazen as brass, and sure enough no one could "learn her nothing." But it isn't she I am thankful for having met—it's the pictures. Oh! such glorious, heavenly pictures—wonderful etchings, engravings, french prints, mezzo-tints—perfectly glorious, scores of them.

I now understand that I am one of the very highly paid persons in the store, and that there has been stirred up quite a lot of bad feeling on that account, and that my particular "buyer" nearly lost her mind over it. If they give her 18 she is certainly overpaid. She has never read anything; she asked me one day if Amy Robshart is alive now, and if she is an actress—we have her picture—and she never heard of Hero and Leander, and calls "The Muses" "Spring." She has about 20 pictures of the Virgin sticking about, hideous things with the Lady's heart hanging outside her dress, and dripping gore. One day a customer—we frequently have very interesting customers—brought in a lovely nude picture to be framed; she had picked it up in Paris, and my lady Boss was so modest she kept it turned upside down on the desk and covered it with paper when taking it to the workroom. She said she felt *humiliated* when handing it to the man who makes the frames.

I love my little "Home"—my free Sundays—my evenings. Ross is a first rate neighbor, we get along ok. We each keep our distance. I am not essential to Ross, and I can exist without him now—I have ceased *to live*—died 4 yrs. ago.

More later. You have my best love—you three.

Jenny

Brooklyn, N. Y. March 9/28

My dearest Boy and Girl:

. . . The only *real thrill* I have ever experienced in my whole life was when I held Ross's tiny hand in mine and knew him to be *mine*. There isn't any experience in life can compare with motherhood—every other experience can be duplicated, or counterfeited, but not motherhood.

What an event it is to have those wonderful teeth in the family, and what a blessing that they have come in March and not in July, for they usually bring fever and disarrangement. Nice, dear little Donald—his pictures are on my dresser (the packing cases) and I kiss them every day.

Jenny

Brooklyn, N. Y. March 23/28

My dearest Girl:

In my opinion Master Donald is a strictly first class correspondent, and his St. Patrick's card to me was everything that is lovely—I just feel in my bones that Donald and I will be friends for many a day. Ross took me to see "My Maryland" on St. Patrick's Evening. It was a long way off from the Emerald Isle, or anything Irish, but was, nevertheless, one of the most charming affairs we have enjoyed in a long time; everything in connection with it was delightful—the music, scenery, lights, costumes—everything.

I am greatly discouraged in my quest for a "job." Of course I am not the only rejected lady given to understand that I'm a back number, a "has been"—but that does not make things any easier. I am constantly on the ragged edge of suspense; I call, when people ask me to call, trot out my *3 references* which cover *20 years,* and then "we shall write if we can place you Mrs. Masterson," but they don't write.

Ross wants me to be a "lady," but again —it's too late. I *don't want* to be a lady.

I send you my best wishes, and best thoughts, every day. The weather will soon be better and that means more out-doors for us all, and we shall delight in watching the green come back in the trees; there isn't much sign of that here yet, but it can't always be March. We hope you are all well, and happy.

Jenny M.

Brooklyn, N. Y. May 17/28

My dearest Girl:

I am still a "lady" except for occasional day or half day jobs in a store; I could not begin to live on what I earn. Of course I could find plenty of work if I want to go out as a maid, or a Mother's Helper who has to cook and wash. I do not think that at this late day I should do that. I have never been a "maid," and have made up my mind that if it ever comes to that I shall take my last trip to the Beach. Life, so called, as a maid would not be, to me, worth living. I could do it if I had a child to support, or someone ill or in distress, dependent on me, but to cook and clean and scrub, merely for the sake of keeping the breath in my body—oh no.

Mothers certainly are a nuisance when they are old, and hadn't sense enough when young to remember that they would not always be young, and I am the champion fool.

Well, this is merely to say Hello. What are you going to do this summer?

My best love always.

Jenny

Brooklyn, N. Y. June 7

My dearest Boy:

Ross is still in his job, and I have almost given up hope of finding any, except I go out as a "maid" and I shall not do that. It's not that I think there is anything wrong about being a maid, but I don't care enough about living to be one. To have to cook and clean and plan for the comfort of a lot of strange people does not appeal to me. I would glory in doing the same things for "my own" but not for strangers.

Anyway I am firmly convinced that I am "through" and ought to step out. I have done all, of any use, that it is possible for me to do in this world. Whether it was for good or bad it is over and done and nothing can change it now, "The moving finger writes, and having writ moves on" and my days for possible usefulness are past. I should step out, but am a coward. To suppose that Ross needs me would be indeed a joke.

Well, more later. There were 4,500 grad-
uated from Columbia yesterday. Some bunch. Don't forget to send
your new address. My best love to you and your dear ones.

Jenny

Brooklyn, N. Y. Aug. 28/28

My dearest Boy and Girl:

What a treat it was, hearing from you so
often in a week, and so much good news about your "loafing,"
and the Darling's picture and everything. You have done me more
good than you know—surely there must be a God, after all. But I
might have known that you would not forget me—you never have
forgotten me, even when you were happiest in your marriage, and
when the Baby was born.

I am again in the Slough of Despond,
and am quite undecided what to do. It has been a question with
me for months whether it was the decent thing to speak about it,
even to you, but at a crisis in my affairs, if I do not turn to you,
then to whom can I turn? One cannot stand alone always. It
seemed for a while that as long as I eat Ross's bread, I should
keep my mouth shut, but—

But it isn't money that stands between
Ross and me—not by any means—it's *women*—more women. (My
writing is awful—I'm all nerves.) Sometimes I wonder if Ross is a
trifle off balance—sex mad. At first he talked lovely about saving
money, building up a character in business and that sort of thing,
and I was in the 7th Heaven. He *has* saved money, it's in our joint
names in a bank, several hundred dollars. That's why I skimped
so. But all the time he was carrying on an affair with a woman, a
Russian Jewess, a very bad affair, and before he got out of it, he
wasn't so far from the Pen. I helped him out of that—

Now it's Marie, the Butcher's daughter
from Toledo. You remember she was (1 term I think) at college
when you were a freshman. You introduced Ross to her. When

Ross ditched his wife he wrote to Marie. It seems she's out on Long Island canvassing books. Ross told me that he had spent a lot of time with her last summer (27) and that it cost him a lot of money, that he regretted it, but he was lonely and had no other place to go, etc. etc. (He had the Kike here in N.Y. but forgot to mention that.)

Well, I believed him, you know, could kick myself for being such a d-f. So when Ross mentioned that she was coming again this year I thought nothing of it. At Christmas he told me that she had written a letter which said plainly that she expected him to marry her, and that when she came to N.Y. she might remain. He then outlined to me a letter which he claimed he wrote to her, telling her that he could *not* marry her, that his one object in life was to make a home for his mother, get established in business, etc. etc. I was surprised when, after all that, she sent him her photo in a frame, and that he placed it on his mantel—he and she in frames—not his mother, or his father, or wife—just he and she—they are there now. She also sent him a book "with *all* my love," but that passed.

Then in Feby. he had the scrap with his Jewish mistress, and had to engage a lawyer. The lawyer isn't yet paid.

Then he announced that Marie was due in N.Y. on July 3. He met her, and brought her out to Brooklyn to see me. I made tea, we had a nice friendly visit.

But the climax came Sunday before last, and Ross and I had a storm.

Ross speaks of renting an apt with say 3 bedrooms and renting one. Marie spoke of coming to N. Y. this winter and renting a room. Ross and I had a scrap—I refuse to do it. Marie will never again enter any house that I am in.

Now, my dear ones, I do not want you to misunderstand. I *do not* object to Ross's marrying, and said so, he is so made sexually that he *ought* to marry. But I won't be a party to a *lie*. If Ross wants to marry either Marie or any other prostitute, all right, I will help to make a plan, and be agreeable, but I refuse to take part in *a lie*. Ross is the *greatest liar* I have ever known.

I did not intend to say so much, but I'm heartsore, and sick, and truly discouraged. Ross cares absolutely *nothing at all* for me—I am a great drawback and burden to him.

Do not send me a private letter, in answer to this, to Brooklyn—send to my name: General Delivery, New York City.

Jenny

Thursday, Aug. 30/28

My dearest and Best:

You will be glad to hear that my little cyclone has, I believe, blown over, for the time being anyway.

But last evening was different. He came home about 8 and was full of news and plans. We talked until after 12 in the most friendly manner, but did not mention the Butcher's daughter. You remember I mentioned our not having rent to pay for September. Well, Ross said that in view of that fact he had decided to pay off his *entire* financial debt to the college, and also clear up the lawyer in the Kike affair. That would leave us entirely free from money debts. I nearly cried I was so glad. That college debt has been a curse to me. Ross does not "remember" just what amount he borrowed from the college— thought it was $150 but it seems it was 200. He sent them over $50 interest about a year ago—5% and now the entire amount, including interest, should not exceed $250. To say that I am glad doesn't half express it. That debt was a disgrace; and *any* debt was a disgrace while Ross spent money on lewd women. I have said to him time and again "Spend any money in any way you choose so long as it is *your own* but you have *no right* to spend other people's money except in case of actual need." I feel very strongly on that point. Of course it is quite possible that he is married to the Christian Sc. old maid, and is merely clearing up his affairs, but I do not feel that he is.

The woman is merely a she-dog to me—the way she has crowded herself on Ross is, to me, a disgrace. 2 letters and a telegram all in one day, and coming to N.Y. ($6.00 for ticket) merely to visit him, and, according to Ross, without an invitation. I am thoroughly disgusted. With her for being so cheap, and with him for permitting her to work him.

If, however, she returns to her native wilds next week, and Ross does what he has outlined to me, I shall ask him plainly if he is married to the beast, if he is I shall not live with him, if he is not I shall hunt up a 2 rm. apt. and do what I can to help him to save money, and to establish himself in business.

He has had enough experience with women to last him for a year or so, and maybe by that time he may meet a woman who is decent—there must be some decent women, even in 1928, but up to this time he has evidently not met any of them.

You have all my best love. I am going out to the Sea now to blow the horror of Ross's women out of my brain and to try to believe that there is indeed a God somewhere.

J.

Thursday, Sept. 27/28

My dearest:

I received *one* letter only at the Gen. Delvy. and have not heard from you since. I am very grateful to you. Had Ross and you had a "confab" he could not have acted more in exact accord with your proposed outline for our arrangement. It was entirely his arrangement to take this apt., it was he who hunted it up and chose it. He has signed a lease for a year, and has given me his word that in that year he will not impose any woman on me, either in marriage or otherwise. Considering the fact that Ross is not financially fixed to marry, I accepted the arrangement for a year. Whether Ross is engaged to the Christian Science woman or not I do not know. I feel sure, however, that if he is still free it is *not* because she did not *try* to bind him. I have no use at all for the woman. Have no use for any woman who solicits men. It is, of course, the style in 1928, and "this freedom" for women to lead in courtships, and in "chasing," but I am so chronic a Mid-Victorian, so entirely a back number, that I feel nothing but contempt for the woman who offers herself to a man.

Ross cares as much for me as he cares for a dead dog, and right well I know it. That I am a burden to him is beyond a doubt, but what can I do? It is rather a disgrace for him to say that he has a mother living but that he cannot get along with her, and that she despises him. The men who knew about our disagreements have not taken his side, and have refused to give him even business recommendations. No decent man could say that Ross has treated me even fairly, much less with any show of affection or respect. If he could say that I was dead it would be fine. I haven't even been a *wise* mother—never was a wise woman in any way—but as my sister said when I was in Canada last time "No matter what you are, or what you have done, you have never deserved such treatment from Ross." She was quite correct. Ross treated me badly. When he married the woman who was to make him "financially independent" was it to *me* he introduced her? Oh No! it was to the professor's wife, his "B.M." (Beloved mother).

Do not say anything in letters to me that I cannot show Ross. If you need to speak to me privately, place the postal date after your signature, very small, and in pencil, and I will call at the Gen. Delvy.

You see Ross never has mail sent to his "home" address. He may have a box, or use his office address. The Jewess lady told me that he explained to *her* that he didn't want "the old lady to see his mail" so she wrote to him to the office. We do not *trust* each other. The Jewess lady was a raging beauty compared to that very ordinary and insipid Toledo woman. No, my dears, I am not happy.

J.

Bronx. New York City.
Friday Nov. 9. 28.

My dearest Girl:

The other night I was pretty near being run over by a car when I unfortunately glanced up and saw the new moon—such a glorious new moon—and I stood stock still in the road in wonderment and delight. I bet the driver swore. I felt ashamed.

And speaking of cars! Honest and true—*we have a car.* Yes, Sah! an honest-to-goodness Dodge—4 cylinder, tourist. It was a used car, but oh! the joy of it. We have only had it 2 weeks, and already have traveled over 600 miles in it. I do hope and pray that you may soon have a car.

Last Sunday we "took in" Bear Mountain, the highest point over the Hudson, and oh! what a view, also the Kensico Reservoir which is New York's water supply, a wonderfully beautiful place.

Ross and I are out almost every evening —many times when at dinner, and we haven't planned to go out, Ross will say "Let's go out for a run" and we just pile the dishes in the sink and away we go—it's lovely. Of course getting the car has put us back in "fixing up" the house, and getting new things to wear, but—what of it? Take my advice, and you know the Immortal William says "a wise man can learn from a fool," and get a car.

How's the Darling? We haven't heard from you for an age but are hoping that no news is good news— you would surely drop a line if things were wrong, wouldn't you?

Were you interested in the elections? We were all "het up." They surely were a surprise. We have a paper here called "The N.Y. Telegram" and its leading columnist is a Harvard man named Heywood Broun. Ross and I think he is the whole thing. Every now and then I keep a particularly good article to send you, and now have several. I shall mail them today under separate cover. Needless to say he does not believe in prohibition, and we were all strong for Smith. That Hoover man, in our opinion, is just less than nobody. Silent—smug—oh! so smug —just like Cal. Gee! I can't bear the sight of that man—indeed, either of them, Cal or Herb.

How far along is our young man now? Does he walk—does he talk—does he climb over everything in sight—is he eating well—sleeping well, and healthy—please send one of his latest pictures.

Best love to all.

J.

Thursday. Jan. 10/29

My dear Glenn:

I am again in the "blues," and turn to you for advice and help, as usual.

Can you tell me if Ross has any matrimonial understanding with the Marie woman? Do you think she expects him to marry her, and when?

My reasons for asking this are because I feel in my soul that he has; he says "No"—but who, knowing Ross, could believe him? If Ross intends to marry I should not be sitting here waiting, and wishing to die. I should have my teeth fixed— they need it badly—*rest,* not mope, get myself and my wardrobe in good shape, and when the spring comes, find a job.

Ross would be much healthier, and happier, if married. He should marry. We would not need to quarrel over it—it is not now in Ross's power to hurt me. He broke my heart long ago. We could make an arrangement, and if he is ever going to marry the woman it's about time. She can hardly be said to be in her first youth. To have people standing around waiting for me to die, is terrible. If I do not die fast enough they may be tempted to hurry me along, and that would indeed be tragic.

Ross lies. He vows he never hears from his "Beloved Mother" (the professor's wife) yet I see letters from her daughter wishing he could live near Mother, now she is alone.

What strikes me as funny is that all of these people completely drop *me* out of the picture. Even Ross. I was merely a "common person" who footed bills—that's all.

> This is confidential—Isabel and you, of course.
> Send your letters to me addressed: General Delivery, New York City.

Jenny

Thursday Jan. 31/29

Dearest Glenn:

If Ross asks you anything about that letter I intercepted—the one about "Mother cannot live for ever —she is not well even now" I think it would be best for you to say that you don't know a thing about it. The fact is you never did see it—there are 4 foolscap pages of it, and the item I sent you is only one of several. The other part is just as bad.

We had a talk about it last evening. No, we didn't come to blows. Ross was surprised and indignant to think that there was anything unkind or unusual about what he said. It was "all right" he said, and that he would say the same things again and sign his name to them and not feel one bit ashamed. That's Ross. But even suppose it was all right, yet knowing that it hurt me, and made me unhappy, I think he might have apologized. However, he didn't. He merely threw the letter on the table, said it wouldn't be me if I were not "kicking up a fuss" about something, and walked out of the room.

This am. he stopped at the kitchen door and said he would not come back to dinner. I told him I would move anytime on 24 hours notice; that I believed he would be much happier and healthier being with a wife or a mistress than he could ever be with me, and he brightened up and said "That's no lie." He is quite willing, he says, to give me an allowance.

My best love and best wishes for our dear ones, and hope that *you* won't get into Jack Frost's grip.

Sincerely,

Jenny

New York City   Tuesday 1/29

My dear Glenn:

I hasten to thank you for your letter which reached me yesterday. The card was delivered by the early mail, and then I went down town about noon and got the letter and enclosures. You mailed the card 15 days ago. I feel no doubt Ross probably took it from the box when passing out in the morning and not thinking it worth while to step back for a second and give it to me, he just went on, and threw it away. That would be like Ross. I was tempted several times to go down and ask for the letter, for of course I doubted Ross, but persuaded myself that I was just bad-minded, impatient, and that you were busy.

The fact is that I am a sick lady—my heart is decidedly on the rocks, and the chances are that Ross won't have to wait so very long until he has the pleasure of sending me to the crematory. The Drs. at St. Luke's Hospital (5 of them) the N.Y. Hospital—the Life Extension Inst. and the Western Union all said that my heart can't last long—it is badly enlarged—and I have high blood pressure. The St. Luke's Dr. went away and brought in another Dr. a dear old man with silver hair who patted my shoulder and told me to "cheer up"—then another Dr. came, and another—they wanted me to have an x ray taken, at the Hospital expense, for "the sake of Science" but I told them they could have me when I am dead.

Ross has a new affinity. She appears to be a very nice girl, he has brought her to the house several times. She is a combination American-Irish-Scotch and has the very romantic name of Vivian Vold. She is in the Art Dept. of T.H.Co. (with Ross) designs silk patterns, combines colors, etc. She graduated from the art school here. She is a blond, very pretty, refined, and quite a lady in manner and bearing—*very New York*.

If he marries Vivian (they are quite inti-mate—he has known her a year or so) I feel quite sure he would urge me to remain with them—do the washing and cooking and the dishes, and cleaning etc. Vivian isn't a lady to do much house-work; but nothing doing—that won't ever happen. No matter who the lucky lady may be, she will have to go it alone so far as I am concerned.

This rigmarole is really intended as a thank-offering for bothering with me—it's mighty good of you. When one has been the infernal fool that I have proved myself to be, one doesn't deserve anything. But, as Ross said, "Mother cannot live for ever. She is not well even now"—and "all things end—Art alone is left to us, The bust outlives the throne, The coin Tiberius."

And:—

"I thank with deep thanksgiving
Whatever Gods may be,
That no man lives for ever,
That dead men rise up never,
And even the weariest river
Flows somewhere safe to Sea."

My love to all of you.

Jenny

New York City   Feb. 8/29

My dear Isabel:

Only that I have been (and still am) in trouble I would feel ashamed for not having thanked you for your Christmas gift long before this. The green plate and stand came safely.

You see, being a narrow-minded, self-centered, selfish old fogey—scared to death because I am growing so frightfully old and still live, I have lost pleasure (if I ever had any) in the importance of plates, and other no doubt very useful and beautiful things.

When Ross had gone to war—Ross, the beloved son of the old philanderer, the professor's wife—he had gone with the old one's photograph which she had given him in a frame, over his heart, on his manly bosom, and she, all tears and fears, for her beloved son—she wrote to me—it was lovely of her to stoop so low of course, she wrote and told how worried she was.

Jenny

Having received news that all her sisters and her brother were killed in an automobile crash some months previously, excepting only one (Betty), Jenny sent Ross to Montreal to be of help to Betty if he could. Though she had been separated from her family for twenty-five years, Jenny comments on the accident as follows:

February 23, 1929

My dearest:

We are quite stunned and heartbroken. Ross will probably return on Monday. Vivian, the nice girl I mentioned to you, is stopping with me until Ross returns. I do not know about the Driver, or if anyone was injured in the other car. Isn't it perfectly dreadful?

Best love to my "Valentine" and you both.

Jenny

New York City   March 22/29

Dearest Isabel:

I have been, and still am, rather a "shook" lady since hearing our very terrible news. Even now I can hardly believe it. My only remaining sister, Betty, is still quite ill—never leaves the house, and may be permanently lame because of her broken hip. Her hip bone is no worse broken than her heart, and life. She is quite without hope, and constantly wishing to die. Considering the fact that *she* has always been the very conservative and religious one of the family it is rather discouraging to find that her religion has brought her no comfort whatever in this terrible slough of Despond into which she seems to be swamped. She fails to see any of the divine wisdom and love of God in that most frightful accident.

Jenny

N.Y.C. April 18/29

My dear Glenn:

It's an age since I received a line from any of you—even my "boy friend Donald" seems to have forgotten me. And I'm still here, unfortunately, and still in my usual troubled condition. Life is truly a curse to some of us.

That he corresponds with the old philanderer, his Beloved Mother (B.M.) and several other "loose" ladies —ladies who know "what life is" as Ross says, I know very well. And of course they come to town, and he has to entertain them. But I never say a word, never ask an embarrassing question. He does not *need* to lie or act double.

The Toledo "solicitor" has no show now, I think. He seems quite taken up with his latest—younger than the solicitor and entirely the Baby-doll type. She has no intellect, but Ross does not care for people of intellect. He knows everything now, what he needs is entertainment and recreation.

Soon as this is finished, I shall go to bed. When Ross marries his present dumb-bell, if he is not already married to her, I shall go back to my hall bedroom.

Are you all well? Are you working very hard? My love to you all, as of yore.

Jenny

Friday, April 19/29

Dear Glenn:

I'm afraid that I am quite a nuisance in shoving my affairs on Isabel and you, but when you remember the compact we made that time I was in Chicago, and all your care over me since, you will pardon. You are my only confidant.

My motive in telling you all this is not to gossip, or backbite, but because I know that when *I* drop out Ross will lie to you and make it appear that things were quite different with us.

He bamboozled Mr. Pratt into believing that he was anxious to support me, would send me a check at any moment, while the fact was that he hadn't $50 to his name at the time, so that if he sent $50 to "support" me he wouldn't have a penny left. He had the Jewish lady on his hands at *that* time. He will also tell you that he has been divorced for 2 or 3 years while the fact is that it is not yet *one* year. He has the papers. The divorce was applied for, but not consummated until last July. He has had his present lady on hand several months now.

The chances are that Ross and I are again near the parting of the ways. He has never cared anything at all for me since he adopted, and was adopted by, the old philanderer. It is as well for him to try his luck again in matrimony—he can then take his other wife to visit his "Beloved Mother" his "B.M." as he did the first one, and they can all be happy together.

I have truly a noble son—an honor to his College, his friends, his family. And all for what? Can it be possible all this is merely for the sake of co-habiting with a woman who sells her body to the highest bidder?

Oh! If he would only settle down for 2 or 3 years and get a footing in business and not always belong to the "floating" population. He is not so very old yet altho' he has squandered 10 precious years. What in the world is the matter, Glenn dear?

I am not a charming person—not beautiful—not clever, but what of that? I carried him in my body for 9 mos. was good to him for many years (you know that) altho' he says I wasn't—that it was all *selfishness* on my part—but even granting all that to be so—I am still *his* Mother. Oh! what is it that's so wrong?

Be patient with me—I try you sadly—but I'm *alone*, and it's awful to be in the dark, and be alone.

I sincerely hope you are all well.

Jenny

P.S. *Do not* write to Ross about me. You would mean all right, of course, but Ross would be very angry, and resent it dreadfully. He says you don't "live"—don't know what "life" is—sometimes I think he is a little "off" and might kill me—he resents your having helped me, and my gratitude to Isabel and you.

J.

Excerpts from a letter written by Ross to Glenn:

April 21, 1929

Your last letter was the one about Mother. I appreciate your interest and your desire to help me that I might help her. And yet, in a word, your letter merely emphasized my own feeling of frustration and futility. I'm afraid there is little one can do, or that I can do, to be a comfort and service of any real or lasting pleasure.

Mother has entrenched herself behind truths, half-truths, and utter fabrications concerning my limitations as the ideal son, and there is no dislodging her. No amount of even demonstrating my presence will change her constant re-iteration that I am entirely bad and have cast her off in her old age. . . . Day and night, Mother recites her own good deeds to her family, her friends, her husband, her son, and how each in turn failed to pay her back. . . .

Ross

May 31/29

My dearest and Best:

No, things have not improved for me. Ross's chip-lady (Vivian) is all settled down in their apartment, about 15 minutes walk from our house, and Ross spends most of his time there—most of his nights certainly for he is seldom in this apt. until *4 or 5 AM* except when he takes an evening off now and then and goes to bed here at 9 o'clock. Ross is so unbelievably unprincipled unfeeling and almost inhuman, that—there is just nothing to be said.

Did I tell you how I found a list of the money they are earning and saving and spending, all jointly of course, also a list of Ross's checks where he paid for her furniture ($250) her rent (45.00) etc.? When I found the list—on May 1— she moved out here on May 1—I talked English to Ross. I begged him to marry the prostitute, and move her into this apt. in my place.

I have not spoken 10 words to him, or to anyone, in weeks. Needless to say that I never even see *the car* now. Ah! Glenn, my dear, Ross is not a good son, nor is he a decent fellow. Ross is sex-mad.

The Chip is of the flapper type—assumes Baby ways, and that sort of nonsense. She might be called pretty, but has no intellect.

There are times when I positively *hate* Ross—he is a contemptible cur. Well, so much for Ross and his present chip.

This morning as Ross went out he said in his cold way—"I shall remain downtown this evening for dinner," and I said "Yes, remain with your chip and come here at 4 am tomorrow." He just went out and closed the door softly. He is too refined a gentleman to slam a door.

Last month he was accepted as a member of the Princeton Club, but I feel sure they would never have admitted him if they knew what a low cur he is.

I am trying to save myself from a Lunatic Asylum, and so am reading my dear books over again—am almost through with Hugo—am fond of him, and then I think I'll "do" some poetry, and mythology—have always been interested in the Gods.

You have my best love, and my sincere gratitude—never forget that. I don't forget how you have always been my stand-by.

Jenny

Excerpts from a letter written by Ross to Glenn:

July 6, 1929

. . . I am sorry not to have something cheerful to say about Mother and me. Our lives seem constant problems—so constant that I am lost in their maze and see neither right nor wrong nor any solution.

Last evening I was told I was mad. And that appears to be a reasonable explanation, though it solves no difficulty.

In a word, this is the situation. Ever since last summer I have returned home to be nagged about Marie. The artist friend, Vivian Vold, whom Mother adopted for four months, helped for a while to dampen the recriminations about Marie. Then Mother decided I stayed out too late with Vivian. Then Vivian moved into a flat, and Mother began throwing my meals at me. "Hell hath no fury," etc. She never talked. She would not ride in the car. Whenever she broke silence at all it was to call Vivian a whore, prostitute, rat, etc., and immediately bring in Grace and Marie.

And this has lasted since April first. Mother sometimes switches to threats. . . . Meantime I am worried about my job which seems shaky, and my life which seems futile.

Meantime I can discuss nothing with Mother who will not talk—nor go anywhere with me. Every attempt boils down to a horrible scene, in which my various sexual debauches are described in the minutest details. I wish Mother would go to Canada to see her sister and friends for a couple of months. It would give each of us a rest. But she won't even discuss such a thing.

Then other times I go to work. There I am the assistant to the General Manager. Politics are trying to oust him. If he leaves, I have no job.

If anything except the passage of time were being accomplished, I would not object. But I get nowhere, have no fun, do nothing, live in struggle of preserving enough sanity to continue supporting Mother and me, and trying to think out a means of living.

If you have a thought about all this, you need not fear telling it. The disapproval of anyone else would seem like praise after my last couple of years—and anyway I hold no thesis of virtue!

Ross

N.Y.C. Aug. 12/29

My dearest Girl:

Well, isn't that fine about your hair? I'm so glad you've had it done, altho' I must say that I am old-fashioned enough to admire long hair rather than the bob. Still it will be a change and you've wanted to have it that way for a long time, and if you become tired of the short way, or find it a trouble, you can, of course, let it grow again.

I am too unhappy to write a decent letter —everything is wrong. Ross lost his position on July 15, he says because of "reorganization"—but—Goodness knows. Anyway, he lost it. Did I tell you that he has had the prostitute-woman in an ap't near us since May 1? He has practically lived with her *all the time* since. Well, now they are away some place *on a vacation.* They have been gone two weeks—I am quite alone.

Sometimes I think that Ross is mentally unbalanced. There is no reason why he cannot marry the creature if he is fond of her, and if he is not fond of her why act this way? He is spending most of his money on her, even tho' out of employment—buys silks, etc.

Maybe something will happen when he comes back—I suppose he will come back, most of his things are here. In the meantime I am getting up at *4 am* staring like a fool at the "roseate hues of early dawn" creeping in between the great buildings—I am often out for a walk at 6. Something must happen. Someone will put a bullet in Ross, or he will murder the chip, or she will murder him, it is all so wicked and wrong. *Why* does he do it?

Jenny

N.Y.C. Sept. 10/29

My dearest Boy and Girl:

When Ross returned from the Cape after his 3 weeks there with his latest "chip," he suffered from an infected ear. The Drs. said "too much sea bathing." It became worse and worse; then a specialist said he must enter a Hospital at once and undergo an operation. He was operated on last week—they found a large mastoid on the inner ear, and an abscess on the outer covering of the brain. It was a very important, and dangerous operation. They now say that if the abscess drains properly he will be ok in a reasonable time, a month or so; but if it grows again, or another forms, they "cannot answer for the result." He has two Doctors in constant attendance, and has every care.

The "Chip" is there—morning, noon and night. She is entered in the ofc. as being "in charge of the case." I am nobody at all. When one of the Drs. told me that he couldn't explain the case to everyone, and anything I wanted to know about it I must find out from "the young woman in charge" I nearly died. Ross assures me that he *is not* married, but it is quite evident that he wants the Chip to do everything for him, and that *I* must be ignored. I do not recognize the Chip when there, but turn and walk out, and Ross seems to think that is as it should be.

I may be able to arrange to leave this house after Oct. 1—the lease will be expired then—I mean to leave Ross—he has gone too far—I would rather be dead than live in this way— But I will let you know.

Ross is doing very well so far.

Jenny

N.Y.C. Oct. 8/29

My dearest Girl:

When making this latest move I was strongly tempted to go to your town and settle there. Of course with the main object of being near Glenn, Donald and you—it would be wonderful for me to drop in on you once in a while, and to watch Master Donald grow up, and I would not go often enough to be a nuisance or a drag—but I believe that if I left N.Y. this time Ross would not send me any money, and that would not be a fair deal. I am not holding Ross up, but I intend to compel him by law, if need be, to at least contribute to my support.

I love Manhattan—have always loved it. I am on 79th Street and the Museum is on 86th, so it's only a step away thro' the Park. Then the Museum of Natural History is on 77th St. almost across the street to the left. I am proud of the house, and the men in livery (am foolish that way) the *cleanliness* of the place, the glorious view—the wonderful air, the hot water—fine.

Yes, Ross's operation was quite a serious affair. He was in the Hospital for about 2 weeks, but is still in the Dr.'s hands. He has not yet found employment, and is not likely to, so long as his head is bandaged.

Conditions in regard to his Chip had become unbearable for me—I *could not* stand any more of it—he has gone to live with her, but that is nothing new, as he has been living with her practically *all* his waking hours, and half the night, since he rented the apartment for her last May.

My best love always.

Jenny

N.Y.C. Oct. 14/29

Dear Isabel:

Ross called to see me last week—he is still in the Dr.'s hands. He looks very poorly. I invited him to return next day and have luncheon with me, and he did—I bought a half chicken (roasted) potato salad, red currant jelly, french rolls, coffee. It was a swell luncheon, and he seemed to enjoy it. You know, dear Isabel, the way to bring Ross to his senses is to *give him what he wants* and then leave him alone.

I wish now that I had left him last May when he moved the Chip to the Bronx. But even if he marries her now (she may force him into it) he will not remain with her long. And that is where *I* come in, and why I invited him to luncheon— so that he may not be *quite* alone until he finds a new chip. Right well I know that he hasn't a bit of use for me—is ashamed of me, and despises me, but still the tie of blood is there, and I cannot believe that he is altogether insensible to it.

Jenny

N.C.Y. Nov. 6/29

My dearest:

You must try and be patient with me for writing so often and so much—it is quite an imposition—but I am in great trouble, *and alone.*

First about Ross:—On hearing that he is living with that woman, and eating her bread—lying in bed mornings while *she* hustles out to work—I was in despair. Of course anyone (except Ross) could see why she does it. She must cajole him into a marriage ceremony—merely to protect *herself*—and *then*—well! then she will tell him what she thinks of him (and who could blame her), just as his first wife did. *She* gains any benefit that is in the dirty business—he loses.

I lay awake the greater part of 3 nights making a thousand plans, and rejecting them. I would save him if I could.

Then yesterday at 3 am it came to me, *a plan*. My plan is this—Ross acknowledged that he would not marry the chip at this time only that he is under a financial obligation to her, and feels that he *owes* her a marriage ceremony. I say, all right, marry her, but *not now*. Today he has nothing at all to offer her. Leave her but announce to her Father and friends that she is his fiancee, and that he is going away to *make a home* for her. Then go, get a job—get himself in good physical condition, insure his life *for her*—have some money ahead, and then say "now here's the home I have made for *you*" and return to N.Y. and marry her. By that time all bills are paid.

I will provide the money—I will pay his expenses to any one of those cities and give him $150 or $200 to start. In the meantime he is not to trouble about me at all—I'll get a job and get along somehow, and *be glad* to do it.

Lady M.

Telegram received November 8, 1929.

ROSS DIED IN RELAPSE. CAN YOU COME?
JGM

Glenn went to New York.

chapter three. 1929—1937

My dearest Boy and Girl:

This is not a regular letter, but even if it were I could never begin to express my gratitude to you. I believe that when two persons really love each other in the highest and best sense of the word, they are never able to express their real feeling in *words*. It must be something felt—believed—understood. That's all.

Tomorrow, or next day, I shall tell you of the happenings here. I have been quite busy and will explain why, and how. In the between times I try to realize what has happened. It is difficult to realize—Ross stood here in my room so very well only a few days ago—it is very wonderful.

Last night when coming home from the Bronx where I went to move Ross's things, and feeling very sad, my eye fell on an evening paper "Princeton 10—Yale 6." In a moment my heart was in my mouth. How glad Ross would have been—how lovely for our beloved College to win again. Only 1 year ago yesterday Ross drove me to New Haven to the game. Everything came our way on that day—we surely were happy, and *one* if ever a mother and son were one. When coming home I said to Ross that even if we were never again to have a happy day together we could at least delight in the joy of having had *one;* and Ross said "Yes, it has been a *perfect* day—if we live to be a hundred we can never have a happier day." He did not know the chip then.

I have something interesting to tell you about the chip—she is surely some chip.

Mr. Barter is a great help and comfort to me. The administration papers were signed yesterday.

My best love—sincere and true to you both. Always as of yore.

Lady M.

N.Y.C. Nov. 25/29

My dearest and Best:

After a while I shall count up all my riches—after the horror of this loss becomes blunted a bit—you know "the years roll by and on their wings bear healing"—wounds do not remain open for always—and then I shall count up my riches—such wonderful friends—*such* friends—the glory of the sun and the stars—the sigh of the sea—the laughter of little children. Oh no, I shall not do as my sister Betty does, sit for 24 hours a day counting the tick of the clock, wishing to go. If ever I want to go that badly I shall go.

Lady M.

N.Y.C. Dec. 2/29

My dearest and Best:

My affairs. Oh, they are all in a turmoil. The chip lady altho' all dissolved in tears, and of course heartbroken, is not too liquid to forget that material things count in this mundane sphere, and lo! she claimed Ross's clothes, and Ross's car, and Ross's name, and it's really funny (I have had to laugh more than once) to hear that old D—f of an uncle of hers call her "Mrs. Masterson Jr." She could not make Ross (poor foolish Ross) marry her while he was alive, and so she wants to marry him now he is dead. Mr. Barter made out administration papers for me and I signed them, when lo! the old uncle came along and protested. He claims that the chip as Ross's *common law wife* is his nearest relative. I insist we must fight that in the court if need be, for if Ross wanted to marry her he could have done so in May when she became his mistress, or at any time since, but time and again he and I have quarreled about it, and he insisted that while she was an all-right mistress he did not want her for a wife. It is certainly new for her to care anything at all about her reputation —too bad she didn't care sooner. However all that keeps us back and we may possibly have a law-suit. If *she* is Ross's nearest relative it is she who will receive that Vet's compensation, and that would be tragic enough to make one die of laughter. She has only known him *6 mos.* February was the beginning of their "great Romance"—dirty and low as they are made—the low contemptible street dog. She killed Ross—morally and physically.

J.

N.Y.C. Sunday   12/8/29

My dear Boy:

No—do not write to the Chip—it would never do. You see, Mr. Barter and I quite ignore her claims, we say she hasn't any. To ask her not to take legal action against me, or to withdraw any action she may have taken, is simply out of the question. She will probably think twice before entering a suit against me.

Well, we found the nigger, it's the compensation, and the car. They won't get either if I can prevent it.

The chip flung 2 or 3 fits—beat the air—beat her head with her hands, and screamed. She killed Ross all right—she beat his head when he told her about going to Chicago—and she killed him.

Lady M.

N.Y.C. Dec. 12/29

My dearest Boy:

We are now launched on the law-suit. Ross left his Vet. Comp'n to his "estate"—I refused to sign the paper acknowledging the Chip in any way. It is now up to her to take action against me for swearing that I am Ross's nearest relative. Wonder if she will dare!

Best love to all.

Lady M.

N.Y.C. Wednesday   12/18/29

My dearest Boy and Girl:

Please ask Mr. Pratt to drop in and see me if he comes home for Christmas; there's nothing new to tell about the suit, except that Mr. Barter has asked Washington (Veterans) if they will waive administration papers considering that the estate is so very small. No answer yet.

My sister will not come to N.Y. for Christmas, so I have offered myself—my services—to the United Charities, as waitress—sandwich lady—or dish-washer—any old thing. I am pretty late in offering, but Betty delayed me.

My best love to you all.

Lady M.

N.Y.C. Jan. 1/30

Glendonabel: Greetings:

I do hope I may be among the first to wish you all a Happy New Year—you have been in my thoughts a thousand times today. Last New Year Ross and I stood on Times Square to laugh at a crowd of young men—very much jagged—who insisted on stopping traffic so they might shake hands with the traffic cop and tell him what a fine fellow he was. Everyone was delighted, and we all cheered for the Police. Today I went to a caffeteria for 20 cents worth of vegetables, and have not spoken two words to a blessed soul all day. Ross wasn't always wise (who is?) but he had only *one* big failing, and many of us have more than one. Had he remained with us he would, in time, have been all right. Poor Ross.

Lady M.

N.Y.C. Jan. 28/30

My dearest Girl:

The fur reached me on Saturday and I am delighted with it. It is quite lovely. Now with my decent coat —it has very good lines—I, at least, am to the naked eye a very respectable, decent lady. Perhaps if some seer could peep into my heart and see the quantity of resentment and *hate* stored there he might forget about the fur and the Franklin Simon lines of my coat and class me with quite another group than the decent and respectable.

Feb. 18/30

My dearest and best:

The car is gone at last—my heart ached to see a strange man slip into Ross's seat and drive away. My poor foolish Ross—my Baby.

That car made me sweat blood. The chip tried to persuade the garage man to give it to her, and when he refused to accept money covering the rent, $38, from her, she threw the money upon the table and went away—he still has the money. It was the new number plates that made my heart drop into my shoes—they cost *13.50*. Well, it's over now—

> "All things end," you know
> "Only art remains to us,
> The bust outlives the throne,
> The coin, Tiberius."

Mr. B. says the car flew like a bird out to Queens, his home, and never a hitch. Ross loved the car. We had a *perfect* day when we drove to the game. A lovely day—we were happy together—Ross and I.

We find, apparently by chance, that the Chip is booked for France—intends to sail on March 4, leaves her N.Y. job end of this mo. She has first tied up the payment of the money, in the Veteran's Bureau in Washington. That's her little "dog-in-the-manger" game, you see.

There is always the possibility—indeed *probability*—that I may drop dead, or be worried to death, or starve to death (she has never heard of that Canadian money—neither did Ross, thank Heaven) and one can't live for ever on air.

Well, she *may* sail, but like the Scotchman "I hae me doots"—I'm thinking she *won't* sail—we have been entirely too easy with her. Now I show my fangs, and I intend to use them and teach this contemptible she-dog a lesson.

Lady M.

Feb. 24/30

My dearest and Best:

At the present moment I am holding my breath and shivering in my shoes—all nerves—waiting to hear

from Mr. Barter that he has served a court notice on the woman
forbidding her to leave the jurisdiction of the N.Y. courts until
our case is settled. I am fearing to be impatient, yet full of anxiety
—but if I do not hear from Mr. Barter within the next day or so,
I shall go down and find out definitely where we stand.

Lady M.

Feb. 27/30

My dearest Isabel:

. . . My Social Service lady and I have
about come to the parting of the ways—I certainly don't like the
Social Svc. ladies. They are evidently out to straighten up all the
tangles in the lives of all of us ignorant mortals, and I just can't
stand them. How this damn bunch ever came to be so wonderful
as they think they are is a mystery to me. I suppose that constantly
dealing with the down and out ignorant class they jump to the
conclusion that they themselves are superior, and truly it "gets my
goat." They just *can't* get away from their job. So I'm pretty well
alone in my Eagle's Nest again, and I'm glad.

Feb. 27/30

My dear:

I really wanted to see you very badly—I
wanted to "talk law"—did you say "Thank Heaven you were out"?
It's this way—when away from my lawyer Mr. Barter I lose faith
in him—he seems to play into the hands of my enemy—to leave
undone the things which he ought to have done, etc.

Last week—*last week* mind you, I re-
ceived a letter from him in which he said "You will be interested
to know that Miss Volt wrote me a very few days after Ross's
death stating in said letter that she realized that her legal position
was hopeless."

When Mr. B. shook hands with me I hated him—I did not intend to offer him my hand. He offered his, and I took it, hating myself for doing it. And then he talked to me—he is such a straightforward, honorable gentleman, anyone should see at a glance that he is a gentleman. And then I was ashamed—ashamed to have doubted him—I don't understand why he does the things he certainly does do, but I can't believe him to be a scoundrel or a double dealer.

You have my best wishes, and best thoughts.

Lady M.

March 6/30

My dearest:

This is the first day since last week (Wednesday) that I have been able to use my lips in either speaking or eating without having them bleed. You can imagine my high fever —deep cracks in my parched lips. I was this way once before when in the Orphanage and we had that scrap about their cruelty to the children. Now "Richard is himself again"—have been sleeping 8 and 10 hours every night, and every time I happen to sit down, either at home, in the train—anywhere.

I am always thinking "Nobody can injure Ross now—Ross is safe, and is all mine as of yore—I don't have to share him with anybody."

Dear Glenn, help me to be fair and just to Mr. Barter—point out to me where I was wrong, if I were indeed wrong. I do not forget that Mr. Barter came to me at the Hospital when the Chip had me put out, and that thro' his coming the Hospital apologised to me, and that I was with Ross until the very last. No, I don't forget that. . . .

Lady M.

March 26/30

My Dearest:

It's only 4 a.m. but I can't stand that bed another minute—am all nerves—wide awake, and mad as a wet hen. Thank Heaven I still have you—what could I ever do without you?

It's all that Barter man—that boob, blockhead—ass. You remember the Bond Co. wrote me re their joint control of Ross's money? Well, I went to my banker and he advised me to get a decent lawyer to take it up with the Bond Co. I did. On explaining the case to the lawyer he squeezed up his eyes and stared at me—he said "So you really had *no case,* it was never in the Courts?" "No." He said "You are not 27—are you?" "No," I said, "nor a chip—I am not a chip." There were several heavy law books on the desk, and he shoved them so hard that they fell with a thud on the floor. He said "It's a damn shame."

As a result of all this I went to the Bond Co. and hunted up the writer of the letter to me. The man just took the file covering my case, which contained several letters from Barter, and wrote "Closed" across the face of it. We then shook hands, and he advised me to go home and sleep and forget it, that I was free from the Bond, and he hoped from lawyers and my other persecutors.

Now it's 20 past 5 and I feel a lot better —you are a help and comfort to me, more than I can ever express. All those terrible years you have stood by me—helped me in every way—no, the world is not so bad.

Lady M.

April 11/30

My dearest Girl:

If my present plans pan out I shall spend Easter with my sister Betty in Montreal. She urges me to go. I believe she will be glad to see me—for once in her life. Well, Betty and I were never very close—never fond of me. She is and has always been strictly orthodox in everything. I am not orthodox at all. To sit opposite each other at 3 meals every day for 365 days holds no joy for me. Nor for her. I must live alone—alone with my dreams—my wasted life—my wreckage. We can be within call when needed, that's the most I hope for.

Then Betty must have money—she lives on her own property, a very nice place, and she probably has cash enough to keep it up. She says she is merely living "from day to day" and doesn't yet know just how she stands financially, but that is what our friend Gov. Smith would call "baloney." She just doesn't want to tell me. But maybe she will want to, after a while. In the meantime I must keep enough to place me in a "Home."

Tell dear Glenn I haven't heard from the Barter man, and if he writes to Glenn regarding me, not to tell him *anything,* until after I am safely under King George's care.

Lady M.

Montreal, Can. April 24/30

My dearest and Best:

This is merely to say that I have arrived safely, and am now under the protection of H.R.H. the King. My coming has been trying—full of tears, heart-aches, and welcomes home. Everyone is kind as kind can be.

When an elderly, grey haired, sad woman with an old and wrinkled face, and stooped shoulders opened our door, my heart sank, for I thought she was the maid and I felt that Betty, my sister, should have come to welcome me; but when the lady took me in her arms and kissed me I knew that she was Betty. I was shocked beyond expression—had I met her on the street I could never have guessed who she was. It is very sad.

We have had a constant stream of visitors since Sunday—men and women we knew when we were all young together. On Sunday our house looked like a Florist's Shop—the very loveliest flowers. Everyone is wonderful.

My best and most sincere love to all three.

Lady M.

Canada   *May 7/30*

My dearest Girl:

. . . She is essentially the same old Betty that she was "when Jenny was a girl," and she drew her skirts aside (literally) so not to suffer polution thro' touching me. Just the same. Her grief has made her old, and stooped, and broken, but her grief is all *for herself.* She misses attentions she has always had.

What gets me is that no one else in all the world has ever known defeat, disappointment, or grief. As for me! I'm just not in it at all. What can *I* matter—who am I? My heart aches when I look at her, she is so broken—but I've got to go out and tramp it off. She never leaves the house—It's nearly two years now.

Lady M.

Canada   *June 8/30*

My dearest Girl:

I have been quite upset, and ill, since coming here, and was, for several days, on the fence about going back. Such a move, however, seemed premature, and so I decided to try the thing out, and rented this apartment. It was a very lucky move—I feel much better already, and am not nearly so nervous. (I'll soon be able to grab my pen properly.) The little excitement and diversion of fixing up my little place was better for me than medicine. Donald's picture smiles at me every day—Ross is on the wall—his pipes and tobacco pouch where I can handle them often—his lounging robe in my closet—it's almost a *home*. My own books, Adrigoole, and Messer Marco Polo, with Ross's prizes, and our gifts to each other, all those things which I love, and are part of me—all here close to my big chair, and me —it's fine.

>All my love to you, as of yore, dear Glendonabel.
>
>*Lady M.*

Sunday. June 15/30

My Dearest and Best:

I had my furniture shipped here—Betty said she would not allow me to have it in her house. So I rented a place of my own, and am now sitting on my own bench, and writing on my own table. And Ross's photo is on the wall, and Donald's on my dresser, and when I cant sleep I get up and make myself a cup of tea, and it's no one's business. It's fine. Oh, no, we didn't fight—I go to visit her now and then—it's much the better way. Oil and water just won't mix.

After getting the papers and picturing that infernal devil leaving Ross's dying bed and rushing to the Bank, twice in one day, to *draw his money;* and I being such an ass to permit her to attend the funeral, or to show her any mercy at all; and then the move—and my grief about Betty, and not knowing what to do—whether to go, or stay—well, my nerves gave out, and lo! I *lost my speech* for two days. One day I couldn't make a sound at all, but the next day I was able to whisper. Am ok again now. Just fancy *my* not being able to speak—truly it must have been some upset to bring about such a state of affairs.

>*Lady M.*

Canada, June 17/30

My dearest Boy:

. . . Poor Ross's ashes:—will you please thank Mr. Pratt in your nicest way for me. I may ask him to do as you so kindly suggest—altho' I would rather *force* the undertaker to carry out my instructions. It was very thoughtful of you to communicate with the express people. I, too, have been to them and they claim that so far as they are concerned the ashes can come through at any time. So I intend to make a statement absolving the undertaker from all responsibility—and have a Notary seal it; then I shall send it with an order to express the ashes. Will let you know the result.

My condition, mental and physical—you are right, my dear, I am a lot better now. Leaving the tony house has lifted a burden from my soul. Truly "Stone walls do not a prison make." I am peculiarly susceptible to "atmosphere"—and having to pass my sister's bedroom door and know that she was locked in with her bottle (bottles) to take, like Mrs. Gamp, "a little when she felt disposed," made my heart behave something terrible—galloping and jumping in my "innards"—

Instead of rushing back to Uncle Sam as I felt sorely tempted to do, I have decided to remain here until autumn, and by that time have made my plans definitely.

Lady M.

Monday   July 9/30

My dearest and Best:

You should be glad to have only *one* great day when you all go "Bang." *We* have Queen Victoria's Day —the day of the King, the Queen, Prince of Wales, Prince George —Orange—Men's Day—Mason's Day—St. Patrick's Day, and the Lord only knows what others—oh! Dominion Day was July 1. Gee! But we don't celebrate by going "Bang"—we close all houses, business and otherwise, and go *dead*—one could not buy a newspaper, a pint of milk, or a loaf of bread to save one's life. We take our enjoyments sadly.

I am *dying* to unfold my great and permanent plans to you, but can't do it until those other things are cleared up.

Best love,

Lady M.

Canada   July 27/30

My dearest and Best:

Everything is all right now—thanks to you, and thro' you to Mr. Pratt. The package arrived yesterday (Saturday) and now Ross is safe with his Mother again—nothing can separate us now—Ross is safe. For the first time in many months—years—I am at peace. Ross is safe. Last night I slept for 12 solid hours, for the first time in many a moon, and don't think I even turned in the bed. Everything is all right. I can't be, or have been, such a wicked person after all—God is on my side.

I have been erring, and short-sighted, and made bad moves on Life's checker board, but I never deliberately *planned* to injure anyone; when full of despair, and feeling that God being disgusted with me had forsaken me (by "God" I mean the Great Governing Power, whatever it may be) then I remembered that Isabel and you were by my side, fond of me, helping me—that I was (and am) *dead certain* of you, and so how could I be so very wicked, how "forsaken"—was I not protected and strong. And so your friendship, and your love, buoyed me up, and helped me to keep a hold on myself. Ross is all mine now.

Canada   August 1/30

My dearest Boy and Girl:

Since receiving that package I have obtained a new lease of life—am sleeping like a top—eating like a trooper, and am full of plans for the future.

Well, the great plan:—Today being August 1, I paid my rent and gave notice—I shall have shaken Canadian dust off my feet, and said Farewell to King George before Sept. 1. The packing co. will take my goods to be crated in about 3 weeks from now—they already have the contract—I pay them before I leave. The goods will be consigned to the Storage Warehouses Inc. who will clear the customs for me. After reaching New York I shall leave my baggage (1 trunk) in the Depot. I shall then hunt a 1 rm. apartment at $25 a month. It's a job, but can be done. It must be clean, and on a decent street—that's all. I can do it in the week that it will take the R.R. to carry the furniture. All I need is a bed, and my handbag, in the meantime—the automats are still on hand.

I shall place the sum of $1000.00 in *reserve* in a bank, and act as tho' I never had it. There will be enough left to help me along. If I live long enough (and the Gods forbid) I shall enter *a Home* and give them the money. If I don't live long enough it goes to Isabel and you, and you will attend to my affairs.

My love always.

Lady M.

Canada. Aug. 10/30

My dearest Girl:

. . . Am anxious to settle somewhere at last—am wondering if I am the Wandering Jew re-incarnated—certainly I'm a wandering something—but it can't last for ever—"Even the weariest river flows somewhere safe to sea."

I shall leave here in the last week of August—will let you know date later so you can watch the papers for a wreck—and then, for a month, my only address will be General Delivery, New York City. Please send me your address.

I could not leave here if I were of the slightest use, or comfort, to my sister, but she has money, and many friends who are much closer to her than I could ever be, and she is in good health, so why stay? I was absent too long to ever again seem one of the family—people should keep in close touch with their own.

Best love to Glendonabel,

Lady M.

Sunday. Aug. 24/30

My dearest and Best:

This is the last word I shall send to any-one, from Canada. My trip to Canada has not been wholly a failure, for had anyone told me 6 mos. ago that my Sister Betty had not been changed at all (except in outward appearance) by that terrible accident, I could never have believed it. Yet such is the case; she is exactly as she always was—selfish, vindictive, mean, self-centered. To her, I have always been the lawless one, the family disgrace, the black sheep *who married a divorced man.* Such horror! I am still the same—in her sight.

Au revoir.

Lady M.

New York City. Sunday. Sept. 7/30

My dearest Boy and Girl:

. . . I had no trouble at all in entering this country—the Govt. man who questioned us at the Bridge was extremely friendly, and my madly beating heart settled down to normal after an hour or so. I don't think it ever occurred to him that I intended to swell the list of the unemployed—I feel quite sure that he mistook me for a "lady."

Go to the Sea for a few days if you can and get away from the placing of furniture and making plans.

There's nothing, no place, like the sea. I've been out twice. Nothing else makes me feel their insignificance—the paltry troubles of living—the immensity of space—the grandeur of God—the strength and power of the Great Unknown.

> My best love to both—"till all friendships die."

Lady M.

New York City   Oct. 23/30

My dearest Girl:

This month has been pretty hard on me —I had to move—it cost a lot—then came Ross's birthday, October 16. Last Oct. 16 Ross spent with me—I watched for him all morning, my heart in my mouth. Then early in the afternoon he came, carrying a lovely bunch of red roses—my favorites—he always got red roses for me. I was in Heaven. He had not forgotten—he chose to have dinner with me—not with the Chip. He took me to a nice place up here on Broadway, and then to a show—a splendid show —he came to my room on the roof, and kissed goodnight under the stars—how little we dreamed of what the next year would bring! I am always thinking of him—always wishing that I had done something I did not do—or left something undone, or unsaid, that I did do, and said.

Lady M.

Dec. 30/30

My dearest Boy:

This is my "ways and means" letter, but let it go until you have a spare hour to think about it—if that happy condition ever occurs.

If Betty dies before I do, which isn't at all likely, I would probably get something worth while, but that is too vague to build on. So the question is, what to do with what I actually possess now. To go on eating it up, as I am now doing, I would soon be without any. I won't do that. I do not want to work. Why work—for whom, or what? To work merely to keep on going, isn't worth it. I don't want to keep on going. Anyway, I've done my share.

So, my plan is to enter *a Home*—a "Home for aged women." A Home for those who are through, and are just waiting. On inquiry I find there are many such in, and near, New York.

Jenny

N.Y.C. Dec. 31/30

My dearest Girl:

. . . Not being a great lover of the new in anything, I cannot bellow with much fervor "Ring out the old, ring in the new"—it is always a matter of deep regret with me to have to give up the old; I love my old dress, and coat, and wear them until they just about fall off.

Well the New is on his way, anyway, whether I like it or not. All things pass.

You have my best wishes and best love for the New Year, and my deep gratitude for the Old.

Sincerely,

Lady M.

N.Y.C. Jan. 13/31

My dearest Girl:

. . . So you see, my dear, I am not really a subject to go out *to work*. To rush out every day on the alarm of a clock, as I have done for so many years, and combat the little worries and vexations, which are bound to occur in any sort of business, would soon land me in a lunatic asylum. It's my mind that is holding me together now—I love the sunset over the Jersey hills beyond the Hudson—I love the hills and hollows of N.Y., love the sea (I go there often), love books—often get away from myself—it's such a rest—forget my terrible failures in life—my agonies—

Well, all that sort of thing points to a retreat of some sort—a "Home for Aged Women." I'm not really so very old, and it's almost a crime to shove myself in among all those decrepit old souls I see in the "Homes," but what else is there to do? And one good point is that I have learned to *live alone*. I can, and have, lived alone so long, that it comes natural to me. I have never mixed intimately with anyone except Ross— have never had confidants until God sent Glenn and you to me.

Lady M.

N.Y.C. Sunday. Feb. 8/31

My dearest Boy:

Sometimes I feel that Ross knows about you and me, and is not far away, and that he tries to help me. If he knows anything now—anything of the days gone by—anything of our heartaches and disappointments, he must know that he made a number of very grave mistakes, and is sorry for them.

You remember that last day he spent with me, and I urged him to take my bank account and go to Chicago, and begin all over again (I told you about it at the time) and I said that the summer months were the most unhappy in my entire life, he got up from his seat at the luncheon table, and walked the floor, his lips white as death, and said "Well, Mod, you had nothing on me." He then went on to say that he knew he had treated me "rotten," and he was sorry, that many times, all summer, he had rushed into excesses, trying to persuade himself that he was happy, but that he knew all the time he was wrong. Maybe he knows now—I must believe that in his soul he loved me.

And so I have been hunting up a "Home." If I become ill here, they will dump me into a hospital, and that will eat up all my money. I have been to see several "Homes," some quite lovely, some little more than a Poor House where the women sleep in a Dormitory. One, a very nice one, has a large stone over the entrance, and cut in it "Home for aged, respectable, indigent Females." Their booklet explains that the home was built when there were only two classes of women "Ladies and Females." Gee! No, I couldn't bear to be one of the "indigent females"—tho' it's a very nice home. I have been out to several places in the suburbs, but have decided not to go to the country. I shall take my chances in N.Y.

Lady M.

N.Y.C. Feb. 11/31

My dearest Isabel:

. . . I am having a great time hunting up a "Home"—a "Home for the aged." It's a joke, for you know Isabel my dear, I am not "aged" at all. Still I must live somewhere, or else take a trip to the roof, for money has wings and flies away.

One place I called at, the poor old ladies were all so decrepit and old that I was ashamed to enquire about entrance for myself, and so pretended I was asking for an "old lady friend."

There's a perfectly beautiful place out in Rye, one of our very select suburbs—the place is like a palace. I might get in there for about 700 or 800 dollars, but it stands alone up in the woods. They are too tony to have a st. car line. The Home is ½ hours walk from the Depot—beautiful auto roads but no sidewalk—where in thunder could I go for a walk? What a horror to find myself at the R.R. Depot some evening in the dark? To be shut up in that place for life like a bird in a gilded cage— oh no!

Lady M.

N.Y.C. Wednesday   *Feb. 18/31*

My dearest Boy and Girl:

It came on *Monday—Feb. 16—*at 5 p.m.— the wonderful Valentine. And what a relief—my heart not only sang like a bird but, as Paddy said, it crew like a rooster. . . .

Lady M.

March 24/31

My dears—Hello:

This is merely a gossip note—so many wonderful things in our papers, and happening every day that I am fairly "bustin'" to talk about them—but there's no one to say a word to—alas!
    . . . If you havent read "The Private Life of Helen of Troy" by John Erskine, get it. It is one of the cleverest things I've read in an age—have just finished it.
    After the Clubs, and several ladies, have decided the present great question as to who invented "Mother's Day" I sincerely hope they may take that person out and shoot her at sunrise—it was some woman, I suppose.
    Love to Donald, and the rest of the family—

Lady M.

N.Y.C. April 3/31

My Dears:

. . . No, I didn't know that the Florists invented "Mother's Day"—our papers have been fighting about it, and some lady in Phila. has taken an action against some N.Y. Woman's Club, over it. I read somewhere that the Florists in convention deplored the fact that they had no suitable ad. as flowers apply to weddings and funerals, births, etc. and one bright member said "Well, at that rate we should tell them to Say it with flowers no matter what—joy or sorrow." Of course the florists make the money, just as the several societies do who sell poppies. But most things in America run to money.

All my love as of yore.

Lady M.

N.Y.C. April 24/31

My dearest Boy and Girl:

It is quite imperative that I should make some arrangement about my future. Apparently I am doomed to keep on going until Goodness knows when—maybe 20 years. Heavens! Since taking to the milk and eggs diet I have grown heavier, feel, and sleep better. But alas! the milk and eggs cost money, and a fortune like mine cannot last long. Then what? The City (thro' the Red Cross) has a Home downtown where they shelter and serve *one meal* a day to 300 girls—18 to 23—who are constantly hunting employment. They are all "white collar" girls. For me to try to compete with them would be worse than silly. I have never been a servant—to start now to wash other people's dishes, and cook, I refuse to do—just to live from day to day wouldn't be worth it. And, anyway, the "Homes" would not consider my application at all had I ever been a "Domestic." Domestics must go to the Poorhouse, or Welfare Island. Not me. So you see my dears I must do something, and soon.

Lady M.

May 18/31

My Dearest:

Your indigent, tho' respectable, female friend is nursing a fractured rib. About 2 weeks ago I was looking anxiously for a letter from one of the Committee Dames, and when noon came I turned in bed to see if one was under my door; the maid slips the early morning delivery under our doors. Yes, there was a letter—now instead of turning out like a sensible person and stooping to pick up my letter, I leaned over to reach it; snap went my rib—I got out then all right, but, like many of the "right" things we do, it was done too late, to save my rib. However, the pain, inconvenience, etc. have compensations for being compelled to rest, keep comparatively in the one position, etc. it not only gave my rib a chance to adjust itself but also rested *my heart.* My heart has been pretty bad for several weeks.

The Indigent females Board meets on Thursday next. After that I will probably know what's going to become of me, and it will be none too soon, for this "on the fence" business plays the mischief with my nerves.

Betty has written lately. She has not yet moved back to her own house and garden, the weather being bad. It is just possible that she may ask me to go there. Her letter may be just a feeler. She is like that.

I will let you know, soon as I know myself. To tell the truth I'm not struck on getting up when I'm told, and eating when I'm told, and having the light turned out at 10. I go to bed about 2.30, and sleep whenever I can. But—nothing lasts forever—all things pass.

Lady M.

May 21/31

My Dearest:

I attended the Board Meeting about noon, and while nothing is definitely settled, I have reason to hope that they will admit me. Their attitude was decidedly friendly and kind. There were about a dozen ladies seated around a large table in what is evidently the Board Room. I fell in love with them all, and whether they admit me or not I shall always be glad to have met them. One lady asked me questions and made notes of my replies. She probably had some form to fill in.

They had, on the table, your letter, one from Miss Groves, and one from Mr. Pratt. They said that no one could be more highly recommended. They asked for my church connection, but I doubt if my lack there will be a serious obstacle. They asked for my family physician. None? Do I mean I have no Dr.? I look delicate, why not have a Dr., am I a C.S.? Would I object to have a Dr. in case of sickness, should they admit me to the Home? Would I undergo an examination by their Dr. before being admitted? Do I incline to C.S.? Then we all laughed, for I certainly don't. Mrs. Eddy is not, and never has been, on my list of friends. If I *must* change to something else, I would much prefer Buddha. I think that my looking pretty delicate and not having had a Dr. puzzled them. But I wanted to impress them with the fact that I am not an invalid, and have no organic disease. They object to sick, or ailing persons. I didnt say a word about my fractured rib.

Well, of course I may never hear from them again, but anyway they are awfully nice.

Best love,

Lady M.

May 31/31

My dearest Boy and Girl:

. . . Well, now *my* news! It is all settled —I have been accepted by the Board—passed the Dr.'s examination, and been assigned a room. The room is being renovated, and will be ready inside of 2 weeks. I shall furnish it myself. It is fine—I am very satisfied, and very grateful. The Board was all lovely to me—the nicest ladies I've met in many a day. They permit me to take in *all* my own things, altho' that is against the rules. So I have bought a nice new Windsor bed, springs, and mattress, sent blankets etc. to the cleaners, and so I shall be clean anyway. They re-paint my room. I have been quite ill over it, but will soon settle down and will then give you more details.

Lady M.

June 15/31

My dearest Girl:

The great step has been taken, and I am now here for better or worse—it's like getting married. I feel no doubt in the world but the step is decidedly for "better" and is the wisest and most sensible step I have taken in many a day.

The house is very large—takes in a block —about 150 "guests," and it seems to me, servants everywhere. I never expected to find so many servants. And they are all *young* —praise be. We have a General Supt.—an Asst. Supt., a housekeeper, several cooks, and kitchen help, several young girl waitresses, 2 men for elevator—a door-man. The meals are fine—white linen—*so* white—and by the way we have our own laundry, and are allowed *16* pieces a week. Isn't that fine. Hottest water ever was, all the time—and the house is *perfectly clean*. It is like a good hotel.

Already I have a protégé—a blind woman. She was head of the advertising Dept. I sit near her at table, cut up her food, watch her, and already we are friends. She comes to my room every afternoon and likes to sit in Ross's chair. She feels the books, and is familiar with them.

I hope it won't be very long before I

have the pleasure of a visit from you. This house is convenient to everywhere, easy to get at.

You have all my best thoughts, and love.

Lady M.

June 21/31

My dearest Boy and Girl:

. . . I will write later and give particulars as to what things I had to sign over to this house, and what reserved. I reserved some, but we shall straighten all that out later on. I am feeling wonderfully well. This is the best move I have ever made.

Best love to all—

Lady M.

Sunday   Aug. 9/31

My dearest Girl:

My dear, my going to visit you this year does not depend on any "plans" of mine. At the present moment I can't eat solid food, not having teeth, and speak with difficulty. The *hole* in my mouth is something awful—like a great cavern, my tongue doesn't half fill it. Well, it will be another month before my "store teeth" are ready, and then goodness only knows how it will be. Surely I would love to go. Donald and I should have met and been friends long ago, but Fate ordains those things, and who can fight Fate? My sight is very poor—frightens me, and soon as I have teeth and can speak, I shall go to a good oculist and get fixed up. It takes money to do those things, but there is no way to avoid it. Of course we have a number of clinics and such, but not for me. I must have the best for such very important work.

Lady M.

N.Y.C. Sept. 4/31

My dearest Boy:

. . . My Dentist and I have had a scrap —the job was to be $100. I paid 50. Before going to Canada last year this same man had placed two bridges for me—$100. But when I got to Canada one of them hurt so dreadfully that I couldnt eat anything, so I got a Canadian to remove it—another $25. Then the 50 paid in June on account, which means $200, and at the heel of the hunt I had nothing at all to show for the money. So I made him return $25 of the last 50, letting him keep 25 for extraction, which I consider a liberal arrangement. There are still roots which must come out. I lost faith in him, so it was best to part. One can find common ordinary people anywhere.

The "Home" arrangement is panning out pretty well. I am glad to be here. There's a feeling of security and finality about it that is very restful. A feeling that nothing more can possibly happen. My room is very comfortable, the food good enough, the house delightfully open, airy and clean, and what more can one want? I have as much privacy as I have ever had, and we are free to come and go as we please.

Lady M.

N.Y.C. Sept. 16/31

My dearest Girl:

. . . You would be interested to meet our bunch here—I find that more than half of our women are "maids" and many of them school teachers, some drawing pensions—75 and 95 monthly. One "miss" has a slim, young figure, but her face! Such a thin narrow nose, and her mouth is exactly like a horseshoe turned upside down—and altho here a very short time she has a lot to say, a self-opinionated impudent creature. When she came first I made overtures, but soon drew back. I dont want to know her.

There's a little old music teacher—used to play the organ in a Brooklyn Church—something fell on her after she entered this house and *broke her back*. She is quite stooped over—her chin almost resting on her knees—it is very pitiful. It is funny how many of them try to "put it on"—one old one told me that her husband was a "Railroad man." She didn't say whether a President, or a porter. Another said her husband was "in the City Hall" in Phila. for many years, and that he wore a tall hat. He may have been Mayor, or a white-wings—the latter wear tall hats on the Labor Day parade.

But I am very grateful to Fate for placing me here—no rent—food enough—laundry—good bath and plenty of hot water—oceans of it—what more can I need. Entire privacy and every evening I can walk two blocks and watch the glorious sunset over the Hudson behind the Jersey hills.

And Ross is safe—no more chips—

Lady M.

N.Y.C. Oct. 9/31

My dearest Girl:

. . . Have you read "The Magnificent Ambersons" by Tarkington? If not get it, it's about an only son, and how his *mother* ruined him.

J.

Nov. 11/31

My dearest Boy:

. . . Ross was near a turning point, Glenn dear; that day he came to me, two days before he died, he said as much. He said his life was "rotten" and he knew it was all wrong. That was when I offered him my bank account—every penny I owned, if he would turn over a new leaf and begin again. He was on the verge of doing it.

The chip *killed him,* you know—when he spoke of leaving her she pounded his dear head, or threw pillows or something at him, and it caused a hemorrhage. The death certificate which came to me in Canada with the ashes says "Cause of death unknown"—"contributory cause a mastoid operation." But he had recovered from the operation.

I can see now why Ross's Doctor, the one who operated, was so "all for me" and professed himself *anxious* to go into court against the chip.

May the Gods be good to you.

Lady M.

Nov. 13/31

My dearest Boy and Girl:

Just a line to say they are too beautiful for words. Perfect in every way—color, freshness, bloom, plenty of green. They actually put layers of oil paper between the blooms to prevent their being crushed. I have never seen more beautiful roses. When Ross spent his last birthday with me—Oct. 16/29—he carried me some roses like those. They have always been my favorite flower, and color; Ross knew that—he loved them too, and so he has never given me any other sort of flower. You are so good and kind to think of me in this way—I appreciate it very much.

It gave me a lot of comfort yesterday to remember that Ross came to *me* on that, his last birthday. He came in the afternoon, took me to dinner and the theatre—we were happy together. I am glad to know that he never spent *any* holiday, any Holy Day, with the Chip.

It is all difficult to understand—let me know some time if you two believe in immortality; I mean in *individual* immortality. Have you any idea what becomes of us?

My best love and gratitude to you.

Lady M.

Friday. Jan. 22/32

My dearest Girl:

. . . The Supt. here, in my opinion is perfectly abominable. I never even say "Good morning" to her. If she ever gets a chance she will steal my things. However, I won't drop out until after I've straightened out my affairs—I am not that kind.

Do I weary you?

Lady M.

Feb. 12/32

My dearest Girl:

. . . One of these days I shall explain to you my attitude toward this house—especially to the old one in the office—the "Supt." but not today.

I have been reading up on American Artists—painting and sculpture—and was especially interested to follow the work of Sargent and Abbey in the Boston Library.

Then I go to the Museum and pick out the things I've been reading about, and find it very interesting.

Lady M.

April 15/32

My dear Boy and Girl:

Whether it's due to the infirmities of old age—that I have become dried up and brittle, or that my bootlegger is supplying bad stuff—anyway, I fell, on Saturday, on the street and fractured a rib. Our nurse here took me to the hospital on Monday—at my expense—and we had an x-ray taken—at least *they* had, for we haven't heard a word from them since. It is now *4 days*. Only that my rib hurts pretty badly I could laugh—4 days to get an x-ray, just think of it! It's enough to make anyone laugh.

You may take it from me, Isabel, my dear, that one never gets anything at all *for nothing*. We went in as charity people—the nurse and I—I was examined by a nice young fellow of about 23, and taken to the x-ray dept. There we found 2 young girls in white, not nurses. They got me on the table, went thro' a number of fool motions, turned a switch. We waited 20 minutes to hear that the young moron didn't get my ribs on the plate—I must try again. They substituted another block-head lady who again went thro' motions measuring me, measuring the plate, etc. We waited an hour to hear that the plate wasn't yet dry, but they believed it showed a fractured rib! They were to mail a statement—its now 4 days, but the statement has not shown up. People must, and should pay for everything they get—experiences, mistakes, service, etc. Nature makes no gifts.

It is, of course, very ridiculous of me to break all my bones one by one—it would be much simpler to step off the roof.

Best love to all.

Lady M.

Sunday   *May 1/32*

My dear Isabel:

        This doesnt look like May Day—the wind is chilly—the rain is a gloomy drizzle, and "God's miracle of May" might be November or anything. When I was a little girl my mother—she "ran" the school—took us all out into the country— and there on a carpet of green velvet dotted with primroses and violets and shamrocks we crowned our "Queen of the May"—it was a great day for us.

New York City   *June 14/32*

My dearest Boy:

        . . . No, I am not particularly depressed —of course life isn't worth living—but I knew that long ago. How- ever "all things pass," and as my dear countryman said "Even the weariest river flows somewhere safe to sea." But you are still young, and are on your way to Norway—Enjoy, and make the most of it—it will always be a glorious memory to carry.
        Dont eat too much fish, or you may be- come so intellectual you will cease to write to me—let the trip be all enjoyment for us all.
        My best love to Glendonabel as of yore.

        Lady M.

N.Y.C. July 17/32

My dearest Travelers:

        By this time you are probably "over there." I have watched the sun set like a glory every evening, and thought that if Heaven made any picture so entirely beautiful as ours over the Hudson and the Jersey hills, surely the picture open to you must be, at least, as grand. It gave me pleasure to know that we were gazing at and admiring the same sun, even if not at the same moment.

You both looked so entirely healthy and fine when here that even if you are shaken up a bit by old Neptune, you can stand it. I watched your boat until the cap, and handkerchief, on deck looked like a fleck of snow, or a feather—I think everyone on the pier was Scandinavian—they are some talkers—and then finally the last 4 of us walked off together. We all cried a bit. I felt very lonely—very much alone.

Lady M.

Friday   Sept. 23/32

My dearest Girl:

It was truly a splendid holiday—and you both look so fine and well—but it is also fine to know that you are again safe and well *at home*. Even if there is a good layer of dust on all the furniture, and one has, like Martha, to be troubled over many things, still it is fine to be home.

Did I tell you about the American who bought a Scotch castle? The big hall with its open fire-place was lovely, and supporting the mantel was a huge flat stone on which was carved "East or West, Hame is best." The American looked askance at that stone, then turning to the agent said, "Now I don't know anything about this fellow Hame—or if it's something to drink, but I know there won't be any advertisements in *my* house." And the stone came down.

Yes, "Hame is best" isn't it—it is nice to be at home. All winter your minds will be full of delightful pictures, and happenings, and you will be refreshed and young (younger) because of the trip.

Lady M.

Oct. 27/32

My dearest Boy:

I have had another experience lately. No, not in the courts. One of our indigent females came to the dining room to breakfast a week or so ago—She was *dead by noon.* It frightened me. For 3 or 4 nights I tossed about without sleep—I, too, may drop out suddenly—my affairs are not in good shape. Ross's ashes was still on the top shelf of my closet—those people here would probably fling it into the garbage box—it would be all my fault. I must dispose of it myself. I went out to Pelham Bay on the Sound, one morning, but lost my way in the Park. I wandered around for hours, found the Sound, but it was all fenced off by private property—I couldn't get near it. I walked, with occasional rests on fences and door-steps, for *5 hours.* It occurred to me that if I went to Coney Island (the places are all closed up now, you know) on a *wet day* I could walk out on the pier where the boats land and there is deep water. It rained on Oct. 12 and 13. I put on storm rubbers, took the ashes, and went. Rain. Rain. On reaching the end of the pier I found *8 or 10 men fishing.* The boardwalk was deserted. There were some beachcombers on the beach, but not many—I wandered on, intending to select a break-water, climb out on the stones to deep water and then— On standing at the rail to look around, a beachcomber—a dirty, filthy-looking ragged fellow made signs to me and pointed under the boardwalk. I actually leaned over the rail to look, feeling sure there must be someone needing help there, maybe dead, or dying —but alas, no. This dirty, filthy ragged brute evidently wanted *me* to go down. There wasn't a policeman anywhere. Certainly I could not now get to a breakwater. And then a man came on the walk. I followed him—he was a respectable looking man—wore good clothing, gloves, carried an umbrella. It was growing late. I touched the man on the arm, he looked at me in surprise; I said "Are you a decent man?" Well, he said that depends on what one calls decent, he tried to be. I asked if he believed in cremation; he said on principle he did, but his wife and family did not, and so he supposed that he would be buried—*but,* he added, what difference does it make when one is dead. He had a strong, nice voice. I told my trouble and asked if he would stand on the beach, hold my purse and umbrella, and protect me from beach-combers while I climbed out on the breakwater. He thought a while, looked grave, and finally said Yes, if I gave my word *not to commit suicide*. The stones were very slippery—green with slime —the tide was coming in and the waves dashed over me, but I went on. The man shouted what stones I should grab. It was done —ah Ross. But I had gone out pretty far—and it was easier to go out than get back. I slipped badly. The man shouted to *sit down* —for God's sake *sit down*. As I knew I could not hold a footing I sat down. The tide dashed over me. The man shouted that I was now wet as I could be and to step down, lift up my skirts and walk in—I did.

He walked to the station with me— helped me wring out my jacket and skirt—there was a quart of water in each shoe—We shook hands—he hoped I would not get pneumonia—but I said that people like me do not die—a young mother with children dependent on her would get pneumonia, but not I. He was gentleman enough not to ask my name, or a thing about me, nor tell his. Now it's done, it is well.

Best love,

J.

N.Y.C. *Dec. 9/32*

My dearest Girl:

It is grand to hear such good news about our dear little man—the gods are not so bad after all. He is evidently cheerful, and active, when he is able to rig up, and run, such a fine ship—maybe some day he may take his poor old auntie M. along and steer his barque to Erin's Isle; that would indeed be a real trip and he could see and smell primroses and violets for the *first time*.

One of our "ladies" went away to spend Thanksgiving with a brother who lives in *a house* on L.I. She tripped on the stair carpet, fell to the bottom, broke her back, got pneumonia on the way to the hospital, and in 2 days was dead. Another, about the same time sat at breakfast in the general dining room, became suddenly ill, and by noon, same day, had gone to the bourne from whence no traveller returns. We have many such cases here. Now all this has shown me the necessity of being ready when my call comes, it may come any day. I am determined to place the things I love where *I want them* to be. I do not trust anyone at all in this house. As time goes on I intend to give away all my treasures—nothing of mine belongs to this house until after I am dead. The woman in our office, the one I like, and trust, least in the house had the nerve to tell me to my face one day that *she* would have my "Byron" when I am gone. Well, she is wrong—she won't. Not if I have any notice of my trip at all.

Lady M.

Dec. 16/32

My dear Isabel:

I have the distinction of having received the *first* Christmas box sent to this house; and I am trusting to your sound sense to understand, and our friendship of so long when I send back part of it. For a person in my circumstances to hoard up things she can never use would be, in my opinion, criminal.

It is yet so early in the Xmas season—not a tree on the streets for sale—that you have oceans of time to send your gifts to some friend who can use and enjoy them.

Now my *real* news. Today is the first of this week that I have been at all nearly normal. I was *under dope* for 3 days and 3 nights this week—I still take it every night. For several weeks I have been annoyed by having my feet "die"—you know that feeling, almost everyone gets it once in a while. I was not at all alarmed, altho' it was queer to find my foot and leg go asleep while I was out for a walk, and of course exercising it. However, I said nothing about it. Then one day in my room my right foot and leg, right hand and arm, right neck and ear, right side of my nose, right side of my lips and *tongue* all fell asleep. Alas! That evening I went to the bath, and when up to my neck in water it started again—my toes first—always the *right* side, up and up to my lips and tongue, my right eyelid even.

The Dr. says it is *all nerves*—no danger, but—I must sleep and sleep and sleep. Hence the dope. 3 days and 3 nights. Today I feel better but walk like a drunken sailor.

Do me a favor, dear, ask your Dr. what that condition is the forerunner of. Is it paralysis? My Dr. says "only nerves". Only nerves, nothing.

You see I feared I might drown in the tub. I couldn't grab the side, couldn't step out because of my foot and leg—I kicked out the stopper with my *left* foot and just lay there until the thing passed. What is it?

Love to all,

Lady M.

Tuesday. Jan. 3/33

My dearest Boy:

. . . Have been "all nerves" since that trip I made with Ross's ashes—used to waken at night bathed in perspiration, feeling the waves dash in my face, hearing the roar of the sea—now I just sleep, and sleep, and sleep—the "twin Sister of Death" for me.

Jan. 11/33

There was a time when you sent money to me to get a Christmas dinner, and I went from one place to another peeping in, and finally came away. I could not bear to go in. It is different now. Ross is better gone, than being here. I am glad he did not have a child. I feel sure he *would not* come back, if he had the chance. He had lived long enough to know that life holds nothing worth living for.

Feb. 6/33

My dearest Girl:

Next time Glenn and you find yourselves in New York—even should you be as kind as to come to my funeral—you must make a jamboree of it, and go to Radio City. Such a place! was there ever such a place! the wonder of wonders —no words could describe it. I went to see Arliss in "The King's Vacation"—it was my first time to see Arliss in 25 years. He is young as ever—gentlemanly as ever—a perfect artist. The entire performance was a marvel—such lights—such colors—such music. You must certainly go to Radio City.

A week ago today something happened to me that placed me back in the Dr.'s hands, and kept me asleep for 3 days and nights. What a blessing it was that dear Glenn did not favor my living in your town, when I was rash enough, and maybe lonely enough, to dream of it, for surely I would be a nuisance to you. My "fright" came about in this way: Every morning about 9 o'clock I go up to the office—Infirmary—4th floor, to get my "dope" for the next night. I am still a sleeper. I found the office door closed, and thinking our head nurse had a patient there, I stood in the hallway to wait for the door to open. Now they have on the 4th floor a maid who is rather a queer looking woman. I do not know her at all, but have several times noticed her quick nervous way of doing things—She is a sort of pantry maid, washes dishes, etc. As I stood against the wall, this maid was doing something at the time at the end of the hall. Suddenly, seeing me, she made one dart at me—threw open a room door, and screamed "Go in, Go in" and tried to shove me into the room. I pushed her away and said *"No, no,* I won't." She grabbed me by the shoulder to drag me into the room, and then we had a *regular fight.* I could only think she had gone suddenly mad, and was determined not to be shut into a room with her. I fought, and screamed, and then the head nurse caught me in her arms, and led me into the office. They got water and salts—the Supt. ran in —I trembled so that I completely lost control of my body. After a while I gasped—"Is she mad"—"No" said nurse, "it's the corpse" —What corpse? Why! the dead woman. What dead woman? My head swam—my heart tried to fly out of my body—they all talked together—were they all mad? Well, it all ended in this—a woman had died during the night, and men were carrying her on a litter to the lift, where we had a mortuary on the first floor; they would have to pass me in the hallway, and the maid having heard that I suffer from heart disease feared I might be frightened, and was determined to save me by pushing me into a room. Between laughter, and tears, and heart jumps, the Dr. came along, and so I'm still here. Wasn't that funny?

     . . . There was a man, one day, very hungry—he entered a restaurant and ordered soup. It was terrible —he tasted it—then dropped his spoon. The waiter stood by and watched the man, saw he wasn't pleased, and thinking to be sociable, rubbed his hands and leaning over said, "It looks like rain, Sir." *Well* said the man it may *look* like rain, but it tastes damn like dish water. Our soup is like that now and then, and as I never eat meat my meals are pretty slim. So I buy eggs, and stuff myself. I feel better since doing it. Having a conscience is a very bad thing, and quite out of style today. Indeed I don't know that it was ever in style.

     Drop a line whenever you can—you are always welcome.

     Lady M.

     N.Y.C. Feb. 26/33

My dearest Girl:

     We have had some changes in our menage since I wrote you. You may remember how badly I back-bit our Supt. and disliked her. To me she was everything con-temptible and mean—a low-born, common creature, and so, of course, being on horseback was an overbearing tyrant. Personally I have had nothing at all to do with her for a long time—I neither asked, nor gave favors. Well, she's gone, anyway. The Board got wise to the lady, and let her go.

Now we have quite a different woman, in appearance at any rate—She is much younger, and knows how to carry her body. She is a Canadian. I only know her to look at, so far—her teeth protrude somewhat, and she seems to be always smiling, and pretty much in love with the world. I haven't much use for perpetual smilers—this thing of "being happy all the day" doesn't appeal to me at all. Even if Fate had placed my feet in a path of roses, I think I ought to remember that there are a lot of other people in the world whose lot is not at all rosy. Indeed we do not have to look very far to find them. We have old women in this house who have fallen and broken their hips—they all seem to break a hip—and who are doomed to spend the rest of their days in bed. One woman has added to her broken hip the loss of sight—she is past 80. So I rather resent my Country-woman's joyous appearance.

Lady M.

Apr. 23/33

My Dearest:

Don't you ever write to the Board, or any member of it, about this house. All our troubles emanate from the Board. To report them to themselves would never do. All our tea and coffee (God save the mark) and all our canned goods are bought from one member of the Board. Would she ever believe (or grant) that the tea wasn't fit to drink? It is to laugh. Another Board lady tells old Mrs. P. she will get her medicine to relieve her heart trouble when she hands over her Bank Book. Ye Gods!

Not feeling well last week I packed my night bag ready to slip out and *run away* if I became worse, for I am determined *never* to go up to the Infirmary and be at the mercy of their head nurse. She is not merely "une Bête Noire." She's a d—— devil.

Lady M.

May 19/33

My dearest Boy:

. . . On the afternoon I went to the Mikado we left the theater about 5 o'clock. I was alone, of course, and felt I just couldn't go back to that house with all those old, old people—old not so much in years—(there are several past ninety) but old in thought—old in emotion—run to seed and decay—so I walked from the theater, 45th Street, to Battery Park, and sat among the bums, and other seat warmers, to watch the sun set over the harbor. And what a setting it was! Water and sky all crimson and gold—a sight for the Gods.

Three-fourths of the women in this house are old maids—I think maybe that is one reason why I am, and always will be, such a stranger among them. They have no memories. . . .

Lady M.

August 27/33

My dearest Boy:

. . . Did I tell you about the woman who died here during the very hot weather and she lay here in her bed, *undiscovered,* until *she decomposed,* and the stench was terrible? She must have been dead *a week.* Of course they hushed it up—it did not get into the papers at all; but are we being watched now? I'll say we are. Their watching has become a perfect tyranny. We are in the dining room at 8 a.m. then the long-legged, hateful, abominable, Y.W. woman, Supt., rushes around sometime between 9 and 10, and checks us all up. I sit here reading—the door open—in she rushes—she's a painfully energetic, active person. "Are you all right, Mrs. Masterson?" she repeats that 3 or 4 times. Mrs. Masterson sits like a log, not a word out of her, not even a look. If the long-legged active creature could hold herself quiet long enough she might see me turn a leaf, but no! When she gets tired asking questions she goes away, and then I close the door, and none too easy.

Oh, those new brooms—What a dust they do stir up in their clean sweeping. This block-head Supt. of ours is a new broom, you know.

Best love to Glendonabel.

Lady M.

Thursday. Oct. 12/33

My dearest Girl:

. . . I have been busy hunting up some class, or lecture course, or something to take up this winter. Sitting around all day is bad for anyone, one soon runs to seed, and that is a living death. There are plenty of classes, and lectures, but they all mean money, and are beyond me.

Of course there are books—we have a splendid public library—3 blocks down—but—they lack the human touch.

My best love to you and best wishes.

Lady M.

New York City. Nov. 10/33

My dearest Boy:

It would have given me great pleasure to be able to accept our dear Isabel's invitation to help usher in your new year, and erect another mile post. But the fact is, my money is low—money seems to be at the bottom of pretty nearly everything.

Sight, to me, is an absolutely essential part in my living at all. People can live and be blind, but not me. We have a woman upstairs (the Infirmary) 86, stone blind, bedridden, yet she eats 3 square meals a day, and lives on. My sight was dim, so I went to *a specialist,* and got new glasses. Specialists cost real money. Then I had an Ear specialist examine my ears— more money—his examination was not satisfactory to me, and so I am looking around for another. I am not exactly deaf, for I hear sounds, but at a lecture cannot follow *every word,* and the movies are mostly a rattle and noise to me (altho' that's not much loss, to judge by the pictures).

Lady M.

N.Y.C. Nov. 14/33

My Dear:

They are perfectly lovely—perfectly fresh and beautiful—in my opinion, a *perfect* flower; indeed their beauty and the love and kindness back of them *did* help to "brighten the day." It will always be a day of wonderment to me —even now it is difficult to grasp—only three days before his going three Doctors pronounced him perfectly recovered—he sat in my room on the roof and we planned his going to Chicago and turning over a new leaf, or rather *I* planned, for he was on the fence. I gave him my Bank Book good for several hundred dollars and begged him to go. He was to come back on Monday—the 3rd day —and tell me his decision, but on Monday he lay in a coma in the Hospital. You say I acted bravely at that time, but it is your kindness makes you think so; I wasn't really brave—I just didn't realize it at all. I have often thought since that it was a mercy I had so many enemies to fight at that time, for I was forced into being alert and had no time to grieve.

I feel that it is quite possible that Ross guided me—Ross in his remorse—or my two sisters who always cared for me—to take what steps I did take at that time to foil the plans of Barter and his friend the Chip.

An old woman belonging to this floor has been ill for several weeks and was taken to the Infirmary, 4th floor. I did not know her very well, but we did say "hello" now and then. When the beautiful roses came on Sunday I felt overcome by your thoughtful kindness, and ashamed of my own attitude in keeping so entirely aloof from those people, so I picked out 5 lovely buds and some green, wrapped them in the nice soft white paper, wrote a short note wishing the old villain a speedy recovery and took them upstairs to a nurse. What happened then? Why, that horrid, ignorant, old wretch shoved them off her bed—the roses and note—"Take them away" she cried "take the horrid things away. She might have waited until I was dead—throw them out." Now, what do you think of that? That is a sample of our "ladies" in this house. Guess I shall keep in my shell.

The coffee served here mornings is just dark-colored water, no odor, no taste—if it's *hot* I feel grateful— When it is merely lukewarm I leave it. And the tea is like lye. So you see, my dear, I've got to have money. When my money runs out, I go to the roof, or a bridge.

Lady M.

Dec. 28/33

My dearest Boy:

. . . I will explain another time why I distrust those people in this house, and why I believe they tamper with the mail.

Seal your letters well.

Lady M.

N.Y.C. Jan. 3/34

My dearest Classmate and Glendonabel:

I hope to be among the first to wish you all a happy New Year under the date of 1934. Health first—good, robust, glowing health, and then after that, anything that is good that comes.

Your splendid box kept me—and is still on the job—from ever having a moment's hunger, in any sense of the word, for when my "innards" felt hollow I opened the box—and when a feeling of desolation—Christmas desolation—fell over me like a pall—I thought of the box and the kindness that made it up, and that helped. . . .

Lady M.

Sunday, March 4/34

Isabel, my dear:

It is quite evident that you have never been an indigent, aged female, or your splendid St. Patrick's Day box which arrived Saturday (March 3rd) would have been more wisely chosen, altho' certainly not with more kindly thought. Possibly you have never lived in one room. This house is largely made up of old women from 75 to 90 something; as a result it is kept unusually warm—very uncomfortably warm for me. I nearly faint in the dining room.

Whatever made you send me *a quart* of thick tomato juice. What did you suppose I could do with it? I always supposed tomato juice was an appetiser, to be taken before dinner, and frequently get it as such when I go down town. It is not appetisers we need here, it is something to eat. Yesterday I went to a restaurant on Broadway, and met 6 of our women, indigent females, all having something to eat. Our meals are a joke, or would be if we felt funny enough to see them that way. When the weather is severe and I cannot go out I lie awake until 3 or 4 am knowing I need food.

But could I get up to drink lukewarm thick tomato juice, or eat very salty crackers? If it were only plain crackers, sweet, wheat, graham, social tea, arrow root, but salt? And by the way, I have never seen them served anywhere—in what way are they used. They would probably be ok with a glass of beer if one had no pretzels or with cold meat. Had the sardines been in individual tins which contain 4 or 5—I often buy them that way—but in such a large tin! I could not eat a whole tin at one sitting, and what could I do with what was left? My room is so hot. I have never eaten preserved meat of any kind—I couldn't. And the cheese is too soft for me.

I hope and pray you will be sensible and understand.

Drop a line and say you're not vexed.

Lady M.

N.Y.C. March 13/34

My dearest Girl:

Ah! I can breathe again—what a relief. You have written, and you are not blazing mad. The Gods are not so bad after all.

You see, the letter was hardly out of my hand when I felt sorry for sending it—you might feel hurt, and be angry and the box wasn't worth that. . . .

Lady M.

April 2/34

My Dearest:

. . . I think I told you some time ago that we had a Supt. who was nothing to brag about, being an ignorant over-bearing individual. Well, like our friend Mrs. Gamp she kept her bottle on the mantel piece, just to put her lips to when she "felt disposed"—she evidently felt disposed too often for the Board got wise to her, and the lady found herself out of a job.

Along came her successor, and why God ever made such a woman is a mystery to me. But then why did he make mosquitoes, or flies or such? This one is a very tall aggressive woman—she has protruding teeth that always make me think of "L'homme de rire," for I never know whether she is laughing or not. But I could stand her looks—not her manner. The dear lady seems to think we are all criminals, here to be taught by her —I was walking down the hall to the dining room one morning— She stood down near the door—"Come, hurry up, hurry up" she said "the bell will ring soon." I might be a puppy, or a naughty child. Needless to say I did *not* hurry up, or enter the dining room at all until after she had rung the bell and said grace. . . .

Lady M.

N.Y.C. Oct. 8/34

My dearest Boy:

. . . That they tamper with our mail I feel quite convinced. Our door-man stands in the hall every meal time and collects letters to be mailed, but instead of walking down the ½ dozen steps and dropping the letters into the mail box placed there he walks into the office and hands them to the great mogul, the Y.W. lady. Why? . . .

Lady M.

Nov. 23/34

My Dearest:

To be so long without saying a word about my beautiful roses, and they were surely beautiful, would be unpardonable only that I have been, and am, "not myself at all" and at the bottom of the Slough of Despond. Everything happened in October and November for me. Ross was born, and died, was killed, then, and my sisters and brother had to go then too. Of course you know the Chip killed Ross—he was going to "turn over a new leaf" and she killed him; even the death certificate says "the immediate cause of death is unknown." It may be unknown to the Doctors, altho' I doubt it, but it is quite clear to me.

Even Isabel's birth, and yours, in those months do not clear up the skies for me. But they do much—how frightful it would be not to have you.

I sincerely hope the day may never come when either of you may feel that life is a curse. Last week I found a scrap of paper in one of Ross's books, and in his writing it read: —"He who in the midst of woes desireth Life, is either a coward or insensible" Sophocles.

I nearly went to the Bridge—roses and all.

I believe that Tom Moore has some artistic value. That is the reason why I sent it to you. Two members of our Board have admired it, and expressed a wish to have it—said to "leave a note in the office about it," well! I won't. No one in this damn prison will ever lay a finger on anything of mine if I can help it.

Lady M.

N. Y. C. Dec. 31/34

My dearest Isabel:

. . . I hope he [Donald] had a fine Christmas. I sat here all alone—very much alone, on reading your letter and tried to live through your Christmas preparations—certainly they were very fine. Donald will have a good many happy days to look back at when he has passed the Santa Claus period.

. . . I have always resented Tennyson's

"Ring out wild bells to the wild sky,
The year is dying in the night;
Ring out wild bells, and let him die."

He hadn't a word of affection, or regret, for the old year—it was all gush for the new. And yet if accounts be true, the old year had given him many little affaires de coeur that must have given him some pleasure. The New Year hadn't given him anything at all as yet.

My best love to Glendonabel.

Lady M.

N.Y.C. February 28/35

My dear Isabel:

My Valentine is lovely—I had just about made up my mind that my love-making days, and Valentine days were about over, and then along comes my lovely "Just for you."

I think that one of the great tragedies of life—maybe the greatest—is when one realizes that life has passed them by—to know perfectly well that nothing very much can possibly happen ever again. My countryman was, of course, right when he sang "There's nothing half so sweet in life as love's young dream"—and even tho' it's only a dream, and suffers many jolts, yet it is everything while it lasts.

What a splendid, ignorant, natural fellow Babe Ruth is—just as God made him—no airs—no pretence—of course we love him, and are glad he is back where he wants to be.

How different a man to that big-headed Swede, Lindbergh, who thinks he knows it all. Of course the trial was a mere fizzle, many of us believe they have the wrong man, and the English and Canadian comments on the trial certainly were not complimentary to America. Such a spectacle could not occur in any country but America. Fancy the puffed-up Swede—an ignorant fellow—and the prosecuting Attorney, and presiding judge (an old fogey past 70) having luncheon together every day

during the trial. Of course the unfortunate stranger was con-
victed. . . .

Lady M.

New York   Friday   May 31/35

My dearest Boy:

This will be my last letter to you from
New York—I leave this prison on Wednesday next—June 5—and
may the Devil fly away with me if I ever again set eyes on it, or on
anyone in it. After I find a place to sleep and have an address, you
will, of course, be the first to hear from me, for I feel sure you are
kind and good enough to feel interested. This "till all friendships
die" is not a matter of mere words to you.

I am not telling this infernal bunch of
grafters where I intend to go—in fact I am not speaking to any of
them at all. On this account it is possible they may write to you
to ask, through vulgar curiosity, where I have gone. You cannot
tell them now, and I trust you never to tell them at any time.
They may possibly try to stop me taking out my furniture, and in
that case I must employ a Lawyer. . . .

Lady M.

Saturday   June 8/35

My dearest Boy:

I am up to my eyes in trouble, and all
nerves. The damn prison refused to let me out, or to remove my
furniture, so I have left—taken French leave—left this morning—
just walked out. . . .

Lady M.

New York City   *July 17/35*

My Friend:

If it were not that my recent experiences have been so very real and so very terrible, my treatment of you, in being silent, would be inexcusable. And you, as usual, were patient, stood by the lower dog, and gave him ("her" this time) the benefit of the doubt.

I must go back to *April 14* when I sent my resignation from this prison to its first directress. She called at my room on *April 16,* acknowledged the letter, said she would place it before the Board, and I would hear from them in about two weeks. The Board meets in this house *every Thursday.* Two weeks went by—four—not a word. I watched them from my window come in and out every Thursday—they simply took no notice of me at all. On *June 3* I asked our Supt. if I might have the use of the front elevator in order to move out my furniture, as I intended to move; she said *no* that the Board said I could not move anything out, and must wait until after their meeting on June 27.

Now the June 27 meeting is the last held until September, there being no meetings during July and August. Of course I saw that was a bluff, they would be "too busy" to get around to my case on June 27, and so I must wait until Sept.

That did not strike me as being fair— April 14 to September 5 is a long wait for an answer to a letter. My intention was to go to Canada, and remain there.

All went well until we reached the International Border, Canadian side. The Customs men came out. Was I going to remain in Canada, or on a visit? Oh, why does anyone ever tell the truth—if some good angel had only prompted me to lie—but alas! I said "yes, going home to remain." That was my Waterloo. They took me from the train and questioned me for *2 hours.* The train went on without me. I must have *four thousand* dollars to enter even on a visit. Needless to say I have never even seen that amount of money. Had I any relatives in Canada —yes, a sister; *prove it*—well, I couldn't prove it right off the bat. The Canadian man was an ignorant Irish Roman Catholic—he

gave me to distinctly understand that I was a liar and a crook. I
became petrified with fright. He refused to let me pass. Well, I
got back to the American side—it was then *1 A.M.*—the American
Customs man was sorry for me. He drove me in his car to a nice
hotel, clean and not expensive—at 2 A.M. it occurred to me that
I ought to telegraph Betty (my sister) and beg her to help me; so
I went out and sent a night letter. She went to the Customs Dept.
next day to see what could be done. They wanted her to sign over
some of her property to me—she refused. She refused to sign
anything. In the meantime I sent an appeal to Ottawa, showing
that my husband *was born in Canada* and that his Father and
relatives owned property there, and I rushed around from one
Customs man to another, until I ached from head to toe.

After *four weeks* the answer came back—
I had lived too long in America to have any claim on Canada—
that it made no difference about my husband being born there
—that I was not in any case a Canadian, having been born in
Ireland, that I was *British,* not Canadian. I could not enter.

How I ever held all the water I drank is
a mystery to me—my lips became so dry I could not speak, and
hadn't saliva enough to moisten them. I was burning up with
fever. Well, there was nothing to do but come back. I had spent a
lot of money—the price of food was shameful, evidently intended
to hold up tourists—it rained for a couple of weeks—I had no
umbrella.

I left on July 3 on a bus. My stars, how
they jolt one! It threw me around from 10 P.M. until 1:40 P.M.
next day—I was sick and sore. I stood like a fool at the Grey
Hound station and wondered where to turn. Was there ever such
a God-forsaken mortal—and what had I ever done to deserve all
that—surely I must have done something, but what was it?

I spent several hours in the down-town
district hunting a room—if I could only lie down. But they all
looked too terribly dirty—old and dirty—better step off a bridge
than live in such dirt—yet I have photographs and more books
that I love, and should destroy before stepping off a bridge—
I must find a room—there must be one somewhere—every room in
New York can't be dirty—I must keep on hunting. When night

came I staggered into a Hotel on B'way, a very nice house. It's a wonder they took me in—I must have looked drunken, but the clerk was a jewel, I told him my trouble, he said "I will give you a room near the Bathroom—slip in and have a good warm bath—then sleep." Ah! It cost $1.50. I slept for greater part of *two* days. Then out again to hunt a room up north. I found one on 149th St. It was evening when I found it. Of course there are plenty of rooms from 5 to 10 dollars a week—nice and clean—but how could I pay that? The first night *I itched* very badly—ye Gods! I was eaten alive—I spent 2 *nights* sitting up on a very hard kitchen chair afraid to lie down—I was ill—real, downright sick, body and soul. It poured rain. I came back to the prison. They must have felt sorry for me—I was nearly dead—they took me in—I own my own bed here—it is perfectly clean—I took a bath, and fell on the bed—what a mercy.

Then my worry began that they might refuse to keep me, but the "release papers" were never signed by me and it's a question if those people *could* put me out; but they didn't try to do it—the Supt. was very kind to me, and said she felt sorry for me.

My clothing is still in Montreal—the Express people are slow in getting it back (with double Express charges) my money came back with double Exchange charges. The Customs people talked of *deporting me to Ireland.* Jerusalem! Fancy my going to Senor De Valera and how delighted he would be with a protestant lady.

Do you pardon me—my terrible silence—my terrible plans that didn't carry? Will write again tomorrow. When you write to me use some sort of seal—a wafer—anything. They open our mail.

My love, and deep gratitude to you all.

Lady M.

July 17/35

. . . Now I *know* one can rent a decent room in Montreal for $10 *a month,* and the 10 I now pay for food would support me there. And what comfort! To make a cup of tea when one felt like it—to read at night when one can't sleep—while here we cannot make tea or anything, and the lights go out at 10 o'clock. I suffer from insomnia, and the nights are a horror. Then, in Montreal I can meet women and men I have known all my life, since we were young together—here I never meet anyone I know, and am too old to hunt up new friends.

Think of being in a city with 7 million men and women and knowing no one. Of course if I were a nice gossiping christian lady I could join some church, but—ah no! For the W. Y. C. A. I have no use at all—like the Y. M. C. A. they are out strictly for money.

On reaching New York I was not only sick and sore in body, but in soul also. After hunting for the room among the dagos and dirty Irish, it became evening, and I was "all in." I had only a few dollars in my pocket—the rest was in Canada—and I was afraid to spend them. The Devil prompted me to go to the Y. W. lodging house on 16th St. They offered me a bed for $1.50 in a room with another woman. I said "I am tired to death—feel terrible," and the woman said "You look it." She then shoved over a form for me to sign. I must become a member of the Y. W. pay 25 cents for the form, and pay 5 cents a day extra while in the house, to show my sympathy with the Y. W. I said I did not want to join—I only wanted a bed. Nothing doing. I would go to a police station rather than encourage such grafters, liars, and hypocrites and I said so. Then I staggered up to the hotel, assured the clerk I was *not drunk,* altho' I looked it, and he gave me a lovely room for $1.50. No religion about it—just business. No hypocrisy—they had a bed to sell—I rented it—that's all.

I never intended to sponge on anyone in Canada—I meant to live on my own money as long as it lasted and when it was all gone to step out of the picture. That is what I must do here. Intend to do. And why not? Who cares? Of what use am I to anyone on Earth? This coming back to prison gives me a chance to destroy things I love, and meant to use in Canada. Some photographs, and a few more books. I will "get my house in order" without delay. Already the extreme weariness and tension has left my body, or nearly so—I can *think* once more. Merciful Heaven, what a tremendous hold I must have on what we call life—my Mother must have been a healthy woman. Best love to you all—more later.

Lady M.

N.Y.C. Sunday   Oct. 13/35

My dearest Boy:

         . . . I have been around trying to hunt up some class, or lectures, for the winter. There are, of course, plenty, but they are all too expensive for me. Columbia charges $15 for the Winter Extension Course, or $1.50 for each single lecture, and when I found they have such lecturers on their program as Amelia Earhart, I pass them all up. The very sight of the woman is disagreeable to me. Then the Met. Museum charges $10 for 3 mos. and all their free lectures are by *women*. I don't like to see women on a platform—never saw one yet I would want to see again, and then their thin squeaky voices give me a pain. I always feel kind of ashamed when I see a woman stand up to speak. Last time I went to the Met. the woman speaker kept *laughing* all the time, and heaven only knows what she saw funny about it, for the subject was on tapestries and their making. Women are like that.

         . . . I have now no hope of getting out of here, and so accept my fate in a stupid, stolid manner as one would if at the bottom of a well. This also applies to many of the half-witted stupid old women who hang around here for years and years—their minds (if they ever had any) have ceased to work, they have gone to seed.

         . . . I am greatly interested in the war and read all the papers, altho' I don't suppose that any of the reports are reliable. It seems the whole world is mad—every line of life in every country is upset. I have now reached the point, like the old Quaker, twirling my thumbs, and nodding at you, say "Except me and thee"—thee will always stand out, and alone, to me. I would be lost without you—I often feel that I am the loneliest woman in the world, but I can never be that while I have you, and that will be "till all friendships die."

Often I do not speak one word for weeks at one time—it is hard to be alone.

Lady M.

N.Y.C. Oct. 30/35

My dearest Boy:

. . . Oh No! you are very kind to offer to cover a class for me, and I'm sure you mean it. But you see, I am not on my last dollar yet, and to accept money from you when I have some lying in the Bank is out of the question.

The Prison   Dec. 31/35

My dearest Girl:

What a faithful person you are—you don't forget—and whether you care a lot for us old fogies or not, you just hang on to us anyway—know it would grieve us if you left.

Your letter—the last this year, reached me an hour ago, and I nearly died laughing about the dog, the dirty creature (don't let Donald know I called him that). . . . I am glad, however, that *you* are not going about dragging a fool-dog, like so many of the "ladies" do here. The way those "ladies" stand watching the fool-dog make his No. 1 and No. 2 on a perfectly clean sidewalk or door-step is too disgusting for words.

. . . May the Gods be good to you in the New Year. I can't tell you how grateful I am to you for making the old one so pleasant for me.

Lady M.

The Prison, March 10/36

My dearest Boy:

. . . One thing I intended to mention in my last I omitted. You will doubtless be surprised to hear that the beautiful red roses which Isabel and you sent me last November are still here on a shelf near the window. When they came I placed them in a vase with water. They remained fresh for a long time, then, like most of us, drooped. I drained off the water, and left them in the vase—time passed—they faded and grew old but were still loved by me. So I just handle them very carefully—don't shake them at all—and there they are. Now and then a leaf falls off, but on the whole they are still themselves, and *you.*

It seems to me that Nature had a miscarriage somehow in you, for you should have been Irish—you have many attributes of the Irish—many of their *best* points—maybe you are like the American Irishman who said he *was Irish,* but was not born in his native country.

Lady M.

The Prison—March 26/36

My dearest Boy:

Certainly it seems that the gods, if there are any, must be fond of green—could they by any chance be all Irish, I wonder! But green is pushing up its beautiful face everywhere now, in every nook and corner—I stood on Riverside Drive yesterday, and gloried over the Park—the Park is terraced—and to look down over the several slopes, all tinged with green is a delight. And there are buds, scores of them, altho' the wind is still chilly. It seems to me there must be something terribly wrong with anyone that does not thrill to Spring—even I, who snoozed and snoozed so stupidly all winter, am almost quite awake again. . . .

Lady M.

The Prison   *Sunday*   *April 11/36*

My dearest:

. . . You can understand, I feel sure (Betty can't, or pretends she can't) that if and when they open and destroy any of our letters we could never know a thing about it. Naturally they would say such a letter never was delivered to them by the mailman, and who could say it was? That they want to know about our money, or property, is beyond a doubt. One old woman was subject to heart attacks and used to beg for a drop of brandy, or some stimulant, and the nurse (the Catholic dog) said she—the old woman—might have brandy if she told what she had done with her Bank Book. The old woman never told. She is dead now.

Lady M.

The Prison. April 13/36

My dearest Boy:

. . . The people who are making a fuss about the lovely green pigs are all wet. The English had nothing to do with it at all, it came about naturally for the pig to represent Ireland because the Irish landlords are all absentees—they live in England—and their Irish estates are let, and sub-let, as a result the sub-tenants seldom had enough to eat and found it next to impossible to pay the rent—so they all keep a pig—they have to be careful of him, if he got cold and died it would be a calamity—so they keep him in the house—the room—with themselves. Every market-day, once a year, he is sold, and the money goes to the landlord, so the pig is called "the gentleman who pays the rint." Of course all the real Irish love the pig. It is only after the Irish become Americanized, and put on airs, that they want to disown the pig.

Lady M.

The Prison. April 15/36

My dear Isabel:

. . . I am afraid my newspaper clippings must be rather a nuisance to you, and I will stop sending them if you say the word. It won't make me angry at all. The fact is I am hungry to death for a little human companionship—if I could only turn to some friend and ask her opinion of such and such an article, or cartoon (I love cartoons) and give mine, but being always alone is hell. The old women here are just sitting around waiting to die. I don't believe any of them give a whoop whether fat Herbert or smiling F.D.R. is elected, or if the "first lady" is merely a wind-bag. And why should they? They are all too near the end of the road where nothing matters.

Lady M.

The Prison. Friday. May 15/36

My dearest Girl:

. . . Far be it from me to wish ill to any poor dog, but I certainly am glad you have decided to banish yours. To have a female dog about the place must be horrible. I spend most of my time these fine days down on the Drive, and to see a fool woman dragging along a she-dog, and all the he's in the place running after them fills me with disgust for both the she-dog and the she-woman. . . .

Lady M.

The Prison   July 22/36

My dearest Boy:

. . . What of me? Oh, I have settled down to the hopeless belief that I am doomed to remain here—barring accident—until I take the Law into my own hands. I speak to no one. What can one say to a stranger of 80 or so, whose thinking days—if she ever had any—are long past.

In the meantime I am trying my best to keep "right side up," heat or no heat, to keep out of the clutches of those grafters and their damn Catholics in the Infirmary, and hope that if there's a God He may take pity on me and get me out of here. But God or no God I can of course step off the Bridge when I get ready. People do it every day—even the young who must have something to live for. I have simply nothing at all—it is almost a crime to go on. A great many of the old ones in this house are more or less "off," and I must act before reaching that stage.

But more anon.
My best love to you as of yore.

Lady M.

The Prison. Sept. 4/36

My dearest Girl:

. . . I have taken several trips to the sea—always quite alone—and while I truly love the sea the coming back—always alone—makes me feel pretty desolate. It's a terrible thing to be old and be alone—as to finding friendship or even companionship in this prison, it is quite out of the question. There is one old woman who knocks timidly 'at my door *every day,* and when I open she wrings her hands in apparent despair, she has mistaken my room for another, or says she has—she is "off" of course. Then they are almost all deformed in some way—many of them on crutches, or hobbling along with canes. We have one old woman of 94. She hardly seems human—all skin and bone, and as they never go out except to the A & P across the street for something to eat, and never read anything except the murders in the newspaper, what in the world could one talk to them about? I seldom open my lips to anyone. Fortunately I love books, and there is a fine public library quite near, and I who rather despise women on the platform, haven't a bit of use for our "first lady," or Miss Perkins, or the fool-widow who roped in the Dane (her third) find real pleasure in our old time books—our George Eliot —Bronte—Jane Austen etc. and the French writers. I have just finished "Of human bondage" by Maugham, and was delighted with it because it shows the futility of life. Maybe you've read it. Of course no woman's life is futile if she has a child. . . .

Lady M.

The Prison   Sunday   Oct. 4/36

My dearest Boy:

. . . Of course it may never be necessary to trouble you about the cremation at all. Betty may succeed in selling her house any day, and will send me enough to enable me to leave this prison—I am a real Miss Jarndyce watching the mail from day to day—always hoping. . . .

Lady M.

The Prison   October 12/36

My dearest Girl:

. . . If I had a daughter I would advise her to marry—marry somebody—anybody—only marry—just to prove that it means nothing. The ordinary "old maid" the good moral ones—if there are any such, merely suffer from sex frustration. Sex plays a larger part in life than we are willing to give it credit for. One of our old maids during the summer when men worked in the garden got out on the fire escape to blow them kisses and smile at them. One tripped on the stairs and fell, I picked her up, and we spoke for a few minutes—her voice has grown high and squeaky—I asked her name, she gave some name, I glanced at the wedding ring she wore, and said "Mrs."? She then explained she had never married, and wore her deceased mother's ring as a protection. I asked from what did it protect her, and she said "Oh the men." She then went on to say that men thought twice before insulting her if they thought she had a husband. Ye Gods! I looked at this extremely plain, unattractive old creature and felt pity. We have now one old soul who, like myself, hates this prison and is deathly afraid of the damn Catholic nurse they have in the Infirmary—she is always running away.

Well, that's the way—there is nothing in life worth living for except money, and one must find that while they are young. If one is so ridiculous as to slip into old age without money one must put up with being crowded into insanity, or "take arms against a sea of troubles, and by opposing, end them."

This isn't a very cheerful Birthday letter to send anyone, but it is all dead true. Save your money, my dear, now while you are young—that's the text. . . .

Lady M.

The Prison   *Oct. 21/36*

My dearest Girl:

. . . It took me a long time to harden me into destroying Ross's photographs, charming letters he sent me from Camp, and France—his gloves and ties—I could only manage a few at a time—but now it is a relief to know that those dogs here can never even set eyes on them, much less use them. . . .

Let me send you my carton of books. Oh, don't say *No*. It sounds terrible, I know, but be merciful to an unfortunate old woman who *loves* her few books—gifts from Ross and his Father to me—mine to them—and send the carton along with your things to storage. If I ever get out of this damn prison you can send them to me, if I don't keep them. They will be happy with you. There are 8 vol. Shakespeare in calf, best paper and print—students edition—good glossary and notes—Shelley in linen—Byron, Longfellow, Tennyson, Moore, etc. etc. all in good order.

I will pay the express charge. I am all nerves, and can hardly hold my pen. It worries me beyond expression. I *have* to get them out of the house. . . .

Lady M.

The Prison   *November 1/36*

My dearest Boy and Girl:

. . . The roses are lovely—never saw any lovelier—the room is full of their fragrance. I do not believe in immortality, but if I did I believe Ross would feel grateful to you. He and I were too close together for many years to be separated permanently by a chip. It is only genuine things that remain. I believe Ross had begun to realize that, and that is why the chip killed him. She probably did not intend to kill him, but was carried away in anger when she felt that she had lost him.

What a strange muddle life is, and why must we go through it anyway—of what use is it?

Your roses—your thoughtfulness and kindness were the only bright spot in my exceedingly dark day, but they were much—thank you sincerely.

Lady M.

The Prison   *November 24/36*

My dearest Girl:

. . . I have decided not to sleep all of this winter as I did last—better die at once. So I've started my study of Grecian history all over again. I've always been a strong admirer of the Greeks—their wars—dramas—literature and art. This history I'm on now starts off on the Hellenes, but that is far enough back for me. Ross gloried in Greek sculpture—many a day when in Chicago I've carried him thro' the Art Galleries on my back—his drawings were later hung at the students' exhibition— he attended the school there. The Art Institute in Chicago is, in my opinion, much more beautiful than the Metropolitan here.

I intend to go to the Metropolitan often this winter—they have lectures, and "gallery talks" almost every day. My reason for not going more last winter is because they are mostly delivered by women, and I don't believe Nature ever intended women for that purpose. They grin and laugh too much— I can't bear "smilers"; we have dozens of them here in this prison —what they find to go about grinning at is a mystery to me.

Lady M.

The Prison   Dec. 29/36

My dearest Girl:

What a perfectly lovely shirtwaist—it came yesterday—you might have heard my "oh" of surprise, there. It is my taste exactly; and the strange part is that it's a perfect fit. Because of my gorilla-like long arms I have always had to buy my shirtwaists too large, otherwise the sleeve would be up to my elbow, but this one is just right.

I went out early on Christmas morning, soon as the prison doors were unlocked, and stayed out all day. The Christmas Show at Radio City was just about perfect, all except the admission price—it always makes me sore to see the prices raised on the very day when men want to take their children, family and friends to the greatest thing in the show line that can be produced. If those grafters were really Christ-like they would *lower* the prices so the whole family could enjoy it. It must be terrible for a father to have to leave out little Johnny or May because he had come to the end of his dollars. No wonder men steal.

I was alone all day—never opened my lips to a soul.

What shall I wish you in the New Year? Doubtless you will get all that is coming to you in one way or another, and that my wishes won't have a thing to do with it. I can only say again with the immortal William "See what is best; that best I wish in thee."

Lady M.

The Prison   Jan. 28/37

My dearest Girl:

Well, this is fine to be in touch with you again. I was lost. The funny thing about it was that it did not seem to me that *you* were lost—it was I, myself. I have been that long without hearing from you before, but could always picture you moving about the big house, or the City—but not *to know* where you were—awful!

We, in the prison, are as usual—the black bow is again on the front door today, and that means another $500 for the grafters. I hope they give the old woman something to eat wherever she has gone, if she has gone anywhere. She will never get sloppier soup anywhere—that's dead certain.

I'm so glad to hear from you—Au revoir— My best love always.

Lady M.

The Prison   Monday   Feb. 15/37

My dearest Girl:

Thank you so much for those splendid postals you sent me—they are fine. It is grand to know that you are having such a wonderful trip. The flowers—so called—came all safe and sound—I am wondering what put it into your head to send them to me. You had evidently forgotten that I am in a prison and have only one cell which faces north west; about 3 every afternoon the sun—when we have any, gets around to my one window. At the present time we have little or no sun because it rains every day, and the first essential called for by the "flowers" is *sun*. Of course you did not suppose that they are something *new* —we had them when I was young, in Canada—Mother was always fussing around with anything that looked like a flower. A peddler sells them on Broadway almost any day that it's fine enough to stand out-doors.

We are not allowed to put anything on our window sills—thank Goodness—if all those ex-servant girls and other common trash got out their eggs and butter on the windows we would be a fine looking sight—so where am I to get the sun for the flowers? My one window is *never* closed—I'm a fresh air, and soap and water fiend. So you see, my dear, the poor flowers have simply no show at all. . . .

Lady M.

The Prison   Friday   Feb. 26/37

My dearest Boy:

. . . I am delighted with the lovely cards from both you and Isabel—they cheer a lonely old prisoner and show she is not forgotten. Life is as usual with me—a sort of living death.

I see by the papers that our "first lady" intends to write a *book,* and a *play.* Ye Gods! Let us hope that neither will be in the least like her "My day" column. She certainly has plenty of nerve. But that is usually the way with women—give them an inch and they take a yard. . . .

Lady M.

The Prison   *March 10/37*

My dearest Boy:

. . . I am glad to hear that Isabel has taken up Art—the only thing in the world that has lasting qualities—

"All things pass—Art alone remains with us,
   The bust out-lives the throne,
   The coin, Tiberius."

Religions pass, governments pass—everything but art.

Many years ago I thought I could learn to paint and attended a class in a Convent (Canada). I painted a canary on a bough, and showed it to my Mother and the family with much glow. My dear sister (she is dead) took it away for a moment and when it was passed around again she had written on it "This is a canary"—I think I cried.

. . . Now be sure and get drunk—good and properly drunk—on St. Patrick's Day, and make your dear mother and Isabel get a jag on.

My best love to you.

Lady M.

Sunday   *April 23/37*

My dearest:

The Hoodoo got me. I fell with considerable force down the subway steps at Times Square—the steps are metal—and broke a couple of small bones in my foot. I was taken to the Hospital for an x ray and am now in a plaster cast. Slept *all the time* for 3 days and nights—feel better now—seems every nerve, muscle, and cord in my body was dragged and strained—am feeling much better now. More later.

Lady M.

May 4   *Tuesday*

My dearest:

. . . They took me down to the Hospital yesterday—a terrible ordeal. The clinic was crowded with all the down and outs black and white. The "boys" merely glanced at me and said to go back in a week. If I were a free lady I would call in a regular Dr. and have him take me to a regular hospital, but the grafters would not permit a regular Dr. to enter this house. We must have theirs, or none. I was afraid to leave the book in my room when going out yesterday—knew they are dying to see it. Examine the envelope and see if you think it was tampered with. I am at their mercy.

Lady M.

New York City   *Sunday. May 9/1937*

My dearest:

I am not feeling so very well—they said I must eat more—I was so weak. I ate more. I bought port wine with your dollar, and am now on a second bottle—it is helping me. We go on Tuesday to have my foot and leg "baked"—it's an ordeal—I may drop out—am taking strychnine to brace my heart. Sorry I could not arrange about the cremation in time. . . . Get cheapest coffin made, no flowers, no minister, no coach. They may need consent of my nearest blood relation; Betty knows about my desire for cremation. Fight for cremation, dear—don't let them put me up in Woodlawn. I have no close relative anywhere but

Betty. It is *you* I trust to protect me. Am not yet well enough to use a pen.

Jenny G. Masterson

Monday   *May 24/37*

My dearest Boy and Girl:

Hurrah! pen and ink once more altho' pretty shaky, but first attempt must be to you.

I think my progress is satisfactory—cannot use my foot yet—but am learning like a baby with the aid of a stout cane. Am hopeful of making great strides this week. At present I am bandaged with olive-oil and straps.

Cannot tell you much yet because I am unable to mail my own letters.

Lady M.

New York City   *June 17/37*

My dear Donald:

Thank you so much for that perfectly lovely card you were kind enough to send me. It fitted in so well with my case that it might have been printed for me.

I am not yet "stepping out" as I used to do but I am a long way on the road to mend. I am delighted to hear that you are again quite close to, and I am sure enjoying, my beloved sea. King Neptune and you are, of course, strong friends—I love him too.

Your little "poem" about the sea gulls is fine—I have put it in my treasure box, as I suppose it's your first attempt in that line. My treasure box holds the telegram which your dear Father sent me when the Fairies brought you to us. It also holds the lace handkerchief which your dear Mother wore on the day she was married. It is indeed a treasure box.

This is my first day out on the street—will write more soon. Am still very nervous.

Lady M.

The Prison. June 22/37

My Dearest and Best:

I have been a very sick lady, in body and mind. Am not yet quite out of the woods, but am on the track to mend. This will be the first of a series of tales of my experience with those infernal hypocrites and liars, and double dealers, the damn Catholics, and the equally damn Y.W.C.A. I dared not tell you much while I was ill because I could never mail my own letters, and of course those dogs opened them.

I was indeed in a bad fix when I found myself at the mercy of those dogs. The Y.W. one wanted me sent up to the Infirmary—I asked the nurse "why"—she whispered "I suppose she wants to hunt for something in your room." That of course means a Bank Book—letters, or money. I begged the nurse to fight against it, and swore there was nothing at all for the dog to find in my room. You would have felt sorry for me had you seen me drag myself along—plaster cast and all—in the middle of the night to rip from the mattress the $30 I had hidden there—you remember! Right well I knew that if the nurse found it, it was lost to me. Everyone in the house knows she steals every cent she can lay her hands on.

Well, one night—past midnight—I lay in a stupor—my room is never dark because of the saloon across the way—I felt a hand steal under the sheet and feel my breasts, neck and back—I was petrified with fright—my foot was in the cast—I was in pain from head to toe—but I struck out hard as I could—pounded her breasts—her head and face—called her a damn dog and other fancy names—and what do you think but she just stole quietly away—slipped out and never said a word. It was the nurse, of course, searching for a bank book or whatever I had hidden. Next morning I apologized and hoped I hadn't hurt her very much—I asked what she wanted, and she said "Just to see if I was warm enough." Oh yeah!

I may not mail what I write tomorrow, but will keep on "confessing"—there's a lot more to tell. Oh! those damn philanthropists and damn "Christians"—how I hate them. Am tired, but don't I write well?

Lady M.

The Prison—Sunday   *June 27*

My dearest Girl:

Soon as I opened your box yesterday and got a good whiff of those glorious pink roses I immediately flew away from New York with its great brick houses like packing cases, and landed in Newtown Park, Ireland. My Mother's sister had a lovely house in Newtown Park, a Dublin suburb—we Gove kids spent a good deal of time there. The house was covered with roses —we drew them into our bedroom windows in the early morning —the dew fresh on them, like pearls. The house was filled with perfume. My love has always been the red rose—but nothing in the world could be more fragrant than those pink roses. . . .

Lady M.

Sunday   *July 25*

My dearest Boy:

. . . Betty writes me once in a while but she has the faculty of writing a letter and saying nothing. But I don't care now—I am practically dead, and to step off the Bridge should not mean much to me. . . .

Lady M.

The Prison—August 5/37

My Dearest and Best:

. . . Yes, I can hobble along now pretty well, but only for a very short distance at a time. I "give out" after 2 or 3 blocks and just *must* sit down. I think, however, that is more due to general weakness than particularly to my foot—I was a very sick lady for several weeks and have not yet fully recovered.

At the present time I do nothing but sleep, drop off to sleep every time I sit down, but I never see anyone and my life (if it can be called life) is terribly monotonous. I don't believe anyone could be healthy and exist as I do. . . .

Lady M.

The Prison. Aug. 26/37

My dearest Boy:

Rain—rain, nothing but rain—not a ray of sunshine for days at a time. As for me, it is hell—after two days continuous cold rain I was nearly starved to death; my daily half potato left me empty as a sack, and I actually *cried* for something real to eat. So I just determined to go out and get it regardless of the consequences, so out I went. It was that terrible kind of rain that came down with great force and then splashed back. Well, I went anyway—did not even carry an umbrella, what was the use? and could not wear a rubber on my bandaged foot. I got coffee—red hot—3 cups, and two eggs. Gypsy Lee had nothing on me. I stood beside my bed and *stripped*—Every rag on my back was wet, and I rung out the rain from the bandage on my foot and leg. I am still stiff from the effects—I suppose cold.

The long days—shut up alone—are pretty long—I never speak to anyone—what can one say to old women of 90, and many of them "off"?

There are two at the table with me—one 94 whose false teeth sometimes get upside down, but she eats along anyway—I try not to stare at her; and another past 80 who hasn't any teeth at all and has her troubles trying to eat. After one says it's raining (and any fool can see it is) there is nothing more to say. I read a good deal—the *old* books—classics—the new make me feel nauseated—we have sex crimes enough in the newspapers. I'm a great old newspaper reader—am alarmed about our friend F.D.R. losing ground—am disgusted about the way the grafters have put Jimmy Walker back so he can steal some more from the fool tax-payer and get a pension—it certainly is a shame—a disgrace to the country. But then Uncle Sam loves grafters.

I seldom write to anyone. My sister Betty being one of the gifted who can write a letter and say nothing, I do not answer at all (there is nothing to answer) unless she sends me a cheque. She hates me, of course (she is a good Christian) but fortunately there is no love lost.

I am doing my best (with wine, eggs, etc.) to become strong enough to walk to the Bridge.

Lady M.

The Prison   *Sept. 28/37*

My dearest Boy:

My dear, no matter how crowded you may be with duties and work, never let me slip entirely out of your life and interests. You have been wonderful to me—I wish I could express how greatly I appreciate it all, and how grateful I am to you. Without you I would be lost and indeed alone. I will try not to bother you too terribly with my little woes, but you are always with me, and I "talk" to you by the hour. . . .

Lady M.

The Prison   Sunday   Oct. 3

My dear Girl:

That was a grand treat—to hear from both of you so soon from the new house, and to know that you have braced up and survived all the inconveniences and worries of the move, and are feeling pretty well.

When mail comes to this prison it is handed in in a bundle to the office, and then is sorted over and examined by the Catholic dog and the Y.W.C.A. ditto. Sometimes, to judge by postmarks my letters are 3 or 4 days old before coming to me. I have always believed (and am not alone in the belief) that many letters are tampered with, but we have no redress—to complain would be foolish, as of course they would deny delaying anything, and how could we prove anything? Indeed if they marked a letter too badly, all they have to do is pitch it in the furnace, and we could never know that it had come at all.

. . . Now *don't work too hard,* take things easy for a while.

My Best love,

Lady M.

Telegram received October 25, 1937:

MRS MASTERSON DIED SUDDENLY GET IN
TOUCH WITH US AT ONCE ABOUT FUNERAL
SUPERINTENDENT

At the funeral Glenn was the only mourner present, though the superintendent and a few inmates of the home attended. Cremation followed.

Death had overtaken Jenny suddenly, at the door of the dining room of the Home. While entering she fell dead—as she had often predicted she would.

From the superintendent's account she had become unbearably difficult. In recent months she had always turned her face to the wall if she encountered any member of the Home in the corridor; had taken to sweeping her dinner onto the floor from the dining room table if it displeased her; and had even attacked one of the inmates, hitting her over the head with a pail. Since everyone was afraid of her—and with reason—the Board had been considering her removal to an institution for the insane.

part two. *Interpretations*

chapter four. from *I*sabel

It is now twenty-seven years since Jenny Masterson died. You have asked me to re-read her Letters addressed to Glenn and myself, and in this perspective to make comments and interpretations concerning her tortured life.

Her Letters bring back many memories, but even in the perspective of years I cannot pretend to discover the key to her nature. Our relationship to her was essentially "neutral." We took pains not to become too deeply involved, but we always answered her communications and tried to help her in emergencies.

Her behavior, like the Letters, was intense, dramatic, and sometimes "hard to take." But to us her nature posed a challenge to understanding. What made her so intense, so vivid, so difficult? Even now her communications arouse in me a sense of the enigma of her personality as well as sympathy for her predicament.

The Letters fall into two parts—the first covering three and a half years prior to Ross's death, the second the eight years that she outlived him. Her focus was lost at Ross's death, for even though there were constant quarrels and separations, she always had the hope of a reconciliation. Just two days before he died, her letter to Glenn (November 6, 1929) includes a hope and a plan—a good plan on paper at least. A few weeks after his death the forgiving mood continues:

Ross wasn't always wise (who is?) but he had only *one* big failing, and many of us have more than one. Had he remained with us he would, in time, have been all right. Poor Ross!

(January 1, 1930)

This conviction she clung to all her life.

They both had strong tempers, quarreling on slight provocation, chiefly about Ross's women—wife, friends or mistresses—his "one big failing." Ross was handsome, somewhat passive, charming and attractive to women. On social occasions we saw him as courteous and considerate of his mother, agreeable to her wishes. They had their gay evenings out "on the town," and occasionally cozy evenings at home.

Jenny had the stronger will and temper, and a deep capacity for hatred. Beyond a point Ross would not accept her domination of his life. Yet after each amorous break-up he would return to Jenny, and they would make a new start, new plans, with new hopes.

Ross was not neurotically in love with his mother. Yet after the failure of his marriage he apparently felt that he could not marry again until after her death because of her intense possessiveness of him and hostility toward any other woman in his life. Such was Ross's dilemma at the time of his death. He was then living with a woman he wished to marry, and she was caring for him during his convalescence from the mastoid operation. Jenny's letter (November 6, 1929) apparently accepts this situation, and she evolves a plan whereby Ross could become formally engaged, get a job and pay his bills, and eventually marry. But before anything could come of the plan he died in a sudden relapse.

With venom and vengeance Jenny turned against his fiancée (the "chip"); and matters were made worse by legal tangles concerning Ross's tiny estate and his ashes. To Jenny Ross's sex needs and sex involvements were the big flaw in his nature, exploited by greedy and designing women. To us as outside observers Ross seemed essentially normal, surprisingly so, given his abnormally close relation to his mother until his college years. His weakness was rather one of ego and character structure, taking the easy way out, accepting what was given him without much feeling of obligation. These traits are easily explained by Jenny's over-indulgence, over-protection, and exclusive devotion to him during his formative years. He was indeed a spoiled darling, but he somehow managed to avoid a sexually toned fixation on his sexually frustrated, dominating mother.

At the time of her death Jenny's only close living relative was her sister Betty (now deceased). Eight months after Jenny's death I found myself in Montreal, and partly out of courtesy, partly from curiosity, I wrote to Betty and she phoned promptly inviting me to tea. This meeting threw considerable light on Jenny's early life and background. I made some notes at the time that have helped me to recall the visit and our conversation.

Betty lived in a pleasant suburb in a brick and stucco house (about $25,000 in 1938) with a sheltered garden, and meticulously groomed lawn. The day I called the rose arbor was in full bloom. She could not afford to live in the house year round as heating was too expensive, so she visited her friends in winter, and they came to her in summer. This contradicts some of Jenny's statements about her sister. She was not rich; she did get on well with her friends; and if she was "set" about the neatness of her house and garden, it was the accepted standard of her culture as well as her personal pleasure.

We had tea in her conservative but tasteful living room. Like Jenny, Betty was tall and straight of carriage but less striking. She dressed well in the style of the day, unlike Jenny who was always immaculate but "turn of the century" in style. Betty was fluent but undramatic in conversation. I felt that like Jenny she was a woman of strong will and opinions. She showed no personal fondness for Jenny, but did feel a family pride and a financial concern for her. Her point of departure was that Jenny was an interesting woman but difficult to live with (a recurrent remark). "Wasn't it a great pity that Jenny was not different so she could have fitted into my home when I needed her." Here she was referring to the tragic accident when her husband and other members of the family were killed. "But I could not call my soul my own when she was here."

Twice Jenny tried living with Betty—first after the accident because of their common loss, and again after Ross's sudden death when Betty again sympathetically offered her a home. On neither occasion did it work out. Betty said Jenny had lived alone too long, was too rigid and old-maidish to accept the intimacies of a common life. Jenny criticized her sister for appearing in her night-gown, for not locking the bathroom door, for having a drink that Jenny did not wish to share. She did not like Betty's friends, nor her pattern of life. She was never made for the role of poor relation.

On her side Betty found Jenny's dramatizations trying, as when she would say, "I am going for a walk in the woods and I may never return. My bad heart, etc." Betty said, "My sister should have written novels or been on the stage. She would then have been a much less troublesome person."

When I asked about their early life, Jenny, she said, was the "odd stick" of the family. Often as a group they would go for walks in the park. Invariably Jenny would walk by herself, pre-ferring her own company. The family's way of life simply did not "rub off" on her, and this is true even though she lived in the family routine, and contributed to its support, until she was 27.

When the father died their mother was left with seven children, six girls and one boy. Jenny (18) as the oldest worked with the mother to support them, but Betty said, "You would think to hear Jenny talk that she alone had worked to support the family." Actually each one took a turn.

Betty asked me one and only one question: "I hope my sister never said anything against our mother?" At this point she watched me like a hawk. When I said, "No, she had always spoken with respect for her mother, admiring her greatly as a woman and teacher," Betty's face softened for the first time, as she replied, "I am glad; she was a wonderful woman." They shared at least this deep loyalty.

I think it important to note that Jenny's mother was ap-parently the only woman in her life whom she fully and lovingly accepted. So far as we know they were congenial, sharing responsi-bility in support of the younger family. With all other women Jenny managed to cross swords sooner or later.

Betty said that Jenny had an exaggerated sense of the im-portance of the family. They were an "ordinary" family, but Jenny embellished them, sometimes untruthfully as when she told acquaintances that her mother had gone to Trinity College, Dublin.

To marry a divorced man was at that time in the Anglican Church equated with adultery. Jenny herself had only a formal family affiliation with the church. I cannot recall that she ever criticized the Church's rule, rather only her brother and sisters who judged her harshly by its standards. Her own philosophy was based on Tom Paine and radical atheistic reformers. In the two years of her marriage we know that Jenny quarrelled with her husband, chiefly about her stay-at-home role while he worked and travelled. In 1896 this was an unusual stand for a wife to take.

With her husband's death and Ross's birth Jenny was free to return to her role of breadwinner. She had a focus for her life that gave her satisfaction as well as purpose: a handsome, intelligent son who became increasingly congenial, willingly guided by her high standards of cultivation. Although she did not attend college Jenny was well read and, as the Letters show, was disciplined and accurate in her diction. During the years of Ross's boyhood she had all she desired in the socially isolated life they led.

But she was also excessive in her material standards for Ross. He was her little prince to be nurtured in an exclusive elegance— "nothing but the best," not only in education and cultural experience, but in physical care. Betty throws light here. When Jenny brought Ross, at age four, to Montreal on a visit, he would eat only delicacies. But after his mother returned to her job in the United States, he lived with his cousins and ate everything and became a reasonable child. As soon as his mother returned he again refused to eat, and she accused the family of starving him, saying that she would scrub floors so that he could have the best, including a pony. She declared she never wanted him to work. Betty thought Jenny completely happy so long as she could do this for Ross and have his complete devotion. "My sister Jenny had a passion for self-sacrifice."

So we know that early in her life Jenny showed some of the factors evident in the Letters: her aloneness, her intense individuality and dramatization, her temper and tendency to quarrel. She was a puzzle to her family, and socially a problem long before we knew her. But to me the enigma is *how* she came to be such a problem to herself as well as to others.

Midway in Ross's college years when other women began to attract him, the quarrels began to disturb their congenial relationship, until finally there was almost perpetual conflict with only occasional hours of congeniality. Nevertheless Ross was Jenny's reason for living until his death—or, more accurately, until the dramatic disposal of his ashes (October 27, 1931).

Glenn attended Ross's funeral and cremation, and spent an uncomfortable afternoon trying to keep peace between Jenny and the fiancée. The funeral service was read in a perfunctory manner by a funeral home chaplain. The whole process was mechanized and tasteless. Even in her grief Jenny sensed its ugliness, and later announced in dramatic disgust that she was "bored." On the way to the crematory Glenn sat between Jenny and the "chip" in the limousine. While the latter was decently silent Jenny kept sending barbed verbal darts across Glenn to her. After the cremation Glenn returned with Jenny to her apartment. For an hour they kept vigil—then Jenny announced, "The body is consumed, now we'll have a good steak dinner." She remained dry-eyed, and ate a good meal for the first time in many days. "After all," she said, "I have a whole lifetime in which to mourn."

In the Letters we note a gradual change. She soon accepted the finality of the termination of her relation to Ross. She had no belief in after-life. Jenny became active again in finding a new way of surviving, even though feeling that her personal life had come to an end. "Ross is safe; no more chips," she writes (September 16, 1931). She proceeded to the business of taking care of herself physically and financially as she always had done.

A month before Ross died, a letter (October 8, 1929) refers to her thought of coming to live near us. After Ross's death she sent us a frank letter of inquiry, and we had to face the possibility of day-to-day intimacy with Jenny.

By this time, of course, we were well aware of her gift for complicating all her social relationships, especially with women. Our friendship would be strained by an endless series of misunderstood actions, flare-ups of temper; and she would have no other target for her hostility than Glenn and myself. We knew that Jenny needed us, but with such a paranoid personality we knew also that our only hope (and hers) was to maintain a civilized but sympathetic distance, with paths of communication kept open. There is no doubt that Jenny's letters had become an increasingly necessary vent for her feelings. Unless she could write them to us her life would be bleak indeed.

So Glenn wrote a kind but frank reply, saying that our plans were uncertain, that my health was not too robust, and in general implying a firm No. We were far from certain how this "rejection" would be received. To our surprise and relief she accepted it without rancor, in fact even with sympathetic understanding, as if she too felt the wisdom of retaining our separation. On this occasion, as well as in scattered places in her Letters, she seems to display moments of self-insight. At times she seems to realize that she is a difficult lady.

And so our correspondence continued throughout the eight additional years until her death, and occasionally we visited her in New York. She greatly appreciated our contacts.

In the last years of her life there was increasing restlessness. For some years Betty had not heard from Jenny. After Ross's death she asked her to return to Montreal to live with her. She came with all her possessions (April 24, 1930), but soon without warning left Betty's home and rented a small apartment. Just as suddenly without warning she left Montreal (August 24, 1930) without saying goodbye and returned to New York. She wrote Betty from the train. To Betty and her nephews and nieces it all seemed queer.

Jenny had a small veteran's compensation from Ross plus a tiny nest egg, and before these slender resources had vanished she was accepted in a Home for aged women, centrally located in New York City. She was delighted with her success in persuading the Board of the Home to admit her, but she soon turned against everything. The food she had at first liked she soon rejected. She detested other residents and was suspicious of the staff. Her paranoid tendencies increased: her letters, she said, were opened and read. Betty had at Jenny's request put seals on her letters but could not resist telling her that she did not believe Jenny's accusation. Betty said, "I was ashamed of the language my sister used—the names she called the superintendent! We did not talk that way at home."

After four years of increasing bitterness she wrote the Board (May 31, 1935) asking to leave, but was too stirred up to await the decision. Unwisely she took "French leave," as she called it, and set out for Canada again. At the border she was stopped for lack of adequate funds to support herself. After much confusion she telegraphed Betty. The requirement of the Canadian authorities was that Betty sign over to Jenny some of her property to insure solvency. This Betty refused to do. With this avenue of escape blocked Jenny returned defeated and forlorn to the Home.

Soon she adopted "the Prison" as her address, and spoke with increasing frequency of "the grafters" (the Board), the "Catholic dog" (the nurse). She had turned against everyone and everything excepting us. On the anniversaries of Ross's death we sent her red roses which she continued to receive with warm response. Occasionally our young son would send greetings. Not much else broke the shut-in pattern of her life, especially after her fall down the subway stairs at Times Square limited her freedom to take walks on the streets of New York that had always been her exercise and entertainment. Escape from "the Prison" was no longer possible. There is increasing absorption with her own troubles, real and imaginary. Her spirit is broken, although to the end she expressed concern for our welfare and gratitude for our friendship.

I have asked myself whether Jenny's personality changed much in the period when we knew her. In her correspondence we note an overwhelming consistency of personal qualities, but also a certain change. Constant was her devotion to us, her only friends, even though at moments this tie too was threatened. Her aesthetic response to nature, to fine arts, especially to sculpture is a recurrent theme. Her fierce financial integrity stayed with her. (She accepted no money from us. On the contrary she sent Glenn $400. to put into his bank account in case she ever needed it. After her death he gave it to the college in memory of Ross.) Her loyalty to her mother's memory persisted, as no doubt her love for her son. She was always exceedingly neat and clean even though monotonously Victorian in her dress and taste in room furnishings. Her need for freedom and independence and her temper were, of course, with her to the end. While Jenny did not have a versatile sense of humor, she certainly had a keen sense of life's ironies, and often saw the ridiculous aspects of her experiences. There were moments of self-insight, although they had no permanent therapeutic value for her.

As she nears the end of her life (she died at the age of 70) the more benign qualities seem to diminish, excepting her appreciation for our friendship. The ugly and difficult qualities become more marked. Her hostility and suspicion turn into full-fledged paranoia. Her appreciations of sunsets, places, art, gradually disappear. Having no philosophy or religion to give meaning to her life she increasingly places upon others blame for her suffering. This self-defeating formula was with her from early years. At the age of 70 she is "the same only more so."

I am glad that Jenny's Letters are now published and available to thoughtful readers. Although her life ended in defeat, in their publication the Letters may win for her a final ironic triumph. By challenging our understanding, and arousing our compassion, they may increase our wisdom, and so in the long run Jenny will have contributed to a bettering, rather than a worsening, of human relationships.

Sincerely yours,
ISABEL ———

chapter five. how shall we explain *Jenny?*

Jenny has told her story. Some outside perspective is added by the two letters from Ross and one from Isabel. The reader now understands the drama—in his own way. Shall more be said? Can we, should we, press further to seek an "explanation"?

The humanist will answer, "No, stop here! Further probing would be superfluous and degrading to Jenny. She has told her tragic tale; now let her rest in peace." A humanist (by which we mean the average reader) has the faculty of putting himself under the skin, in the heart, and in the muscles of another, and of reacting in his mind as the other would. Can we improve on humanism, on the art of empathy?

Perhaps not, but unfortunately, the psychologist has a curiosity that drives him further, sometimes even to the point of indelicacy. He wishes to grasp not merely the *what* of Jenny but also the *why*. Jenny does not tell why she behaves in such a self-defeating manner. The psychologist wants to know.

Throughout the ages the riddle of individuality has been explored by the giants of literature. Tardily the psychologist arrives on the scene (someone has said, two thousand years too late). To some humanists he looks like a conceited intruder. One critic complains that when psychology deals with human personality it says only what literature has always said, but says it less artfully.

It would be a pedant indeed who would prefer the collections of facts and strings of abstractions that psychology offers to the vivid portraits presented by gifted writers, Jenny included. The literary artist creates his account; the psychologist merely compiles his. Psychological forceps seem too coarse to grasp the realities, the subtleties, and unities of a concrete human life.

Goaded by such taunts the psychologist defends himself. Literary portraits, he retorts, are marked by arbitrary selection, by subjective bias, and often by special pleading. Autobiographical documents, such as Jenny has written, seem always to justify the narrator. Objective reality is disfigured. The literary writer feels justified in piling up his biases and his undisciplined metaphors so long as they entertain his readers. A psychologist is not permitted to be entertaining. (He is suspect if he is even interesting.) To be considered valid his analysis must be firmly grounded in evidence and must command the assent of other trained observers.

But it is not profitable to prolong the quarrel. The simple truth is that two authentic methods exist for the study of human personality—one in literature, the other in the science of psychology. A student of human character does well to follow both pathways.[1]

SCIENCE AND THE SINGLE CASE

The two methods correspond to the two modes of interest and attention of which the human mind is capable. The mind may classify its experiences and contemplate the general laws that emerge, or it may be concerned with the individual pattern of an experience. In a well-known passage William James draws this distinction.

The first thing the intellect does with an object is to class it along with something else. But any object that is infinitely important to us and awakens our devotion feels to us also as if it must be *sui generis* and unique. Probably a crab would be filled with a sense of personal outrage if it could hear us class it without ado or apology as a crustacean, and thus dispose of it. "I am no such thing," it would say; "*I am myself, myself alone.*"[2]

Many philosophers have noted the opposition between the two types of knowledge. Bergson contrasts *analysis* (the scientific attitude) and *intuition* (the immediate common-sense attitude). Many German philosophers are intrigued by the distinction. They sometimes speak of *nomothetic* (general) knowledge as opposed to *idiographic* knowledge (of the particular event). It is obvious that the former characteristically leads to scientific knowledge and the latter to literary or historical knowledge. In the field of personality Dilthey and Spranger believe that the first (analytical type of knowledge) is never sufficient. "We *explain* nature," writes Dilthey, "but we *understand* persons." This point of view has led to a whole school of psychology (as a *Geisteswissenschaft*) whose primary method is understanding (*Verstehen*).[3]

Now the question arises as to whether understanding the single case (Jenny) can be fitted to the requirements of scientific method. Many psychologists would say No. Individual cases, they argue, are quite out of place in science unless they can be combined and generalized into types from which general laws can be derived. *Scientia non est individuorum.*

And yet the problem is not so simple. Jenny, like any single concrete personality, is a specimen of human nature, but so individual and unique that we are forced to seek the structures and laws of her own being. To be sure she partakes of our general human nature; but she seems to have also a lawful regularity in her own peculiar pattern of life.

Now the goals of science are to understand, predict, and control events. How, in dealing with a concrete person, can we expect to understand, predict, control, unless we know the individual pattern and not merely the universal tendencies of the human mind-in-general? (A man who wishes to please his wife with a Christmas gift does less well if he relies on his knowledge of feminine psychology in general than if he knows the individual desires and tastes of his wife.) Thus we need not only *dimensional* knowledge (that cuts across all people) but also *morphogenic* knowledge concerning the way in which a given life takes on its unique shape and form.[4] Such clinical understanding is not outside the orbit of psychological science, but well within it.

No need to prolong this methodological dispute. Our task is to explain as best we can Jenny's tangled life. In so doing we shall draw on both dimensional and morphogenic lines of evidence wherever they seem helpful.

PSYCHOLOGICAL APPROACHES TO JENNY

An obvious objection to "psychologizing" Jenny is that we do not have full information. Our available knowledge other than the Letters is sketchy, and nothing at all is known of her infancy —from the point of view of psychoanalysis a fatal barrier to explanation. We regret the lack, and because of it shall do well to hold our interpretations lightly.

And yet the plea "not enough information" may reflect defensiveness. Just as a poor workman blames his tools, so do we, when baffled by a case study, tend to say that the tool of information is at fault. Wistfully we hope that some missing fragment of information will magically solve the whole riddle. And in a culture that stresses environmentalism and is child-centered, we suspect that the early life holds the golden key.

Yet if we had more extensive developmental information we might still be baffled. We might then shift the onus onto heredity. Could an unhappy crossing of genes have produced Jenny's misanthropy? Perhaps so, but merely to ask this question is to remind ourselves how vast is our ignorance of human genetics in general, not to speak of the genetics of any individual in particular.

All this means that our hopes should not be too high. We are starting with a literary self-portrait, excellent in its own genre. Our task is to see whether psychological analysis can add to our understanding (and explanation) of the life depicted.

Available to us is a large store of psychological theories, speculations, and modes of analysis. After sifting them through we discover three types of approach that hold special promise for the case at hand. We shall label them (1) the *existential* approach, (2) the *depth* approach, and (3) the *structural-dynamic* approach. A separate chapter is devoted to each.

All three contain helpful insights, although none alone seems to give complete conceptual anchorage for our explanation of Jenny. Some readers may find one approach most convincing, some another. Our ultimate task is to select and blend the truth that lies in all three.

NOTES

1. Among autobiographical documents that seem, like Jenny's Letters, to have special value for psychological analysis we may list the following: W. E. Leonard, *The Locomotive God*. New York: Century, 1927; H. G. Wells, *Experiment in Autobiography*. New York: Macmillan, 1934. O. Lewis (ed.), *The Children of Sanchez*, New York: Random House, 1963. B. Kaplan (ed.), *The Inner World of Mental Illness*, New York: Harper & Row, 1964.

The intimate relationship between psychology and literature is brought out by Gloria B. Levitas (ed.), in *The World of Psychology*. New York: Braziller, 1963. 2 vols.

A volume that applies psychological methods to the study of individual personalities is R. W. White (ed.), *The Study of Lives: Essays on Personality in Honor of Henry A. Murray*. New York: Atherton Press, 1963.

2. W. James, *The Varieties of Religious Experience*. New York: Modern Library, p. 10.

3. A fuller development of this point, as well as a comprehensive discussion of the utilization of first-person material, may be found in G. W. Allport, *The Use of Personal Documents in Psychological Science*. New York: Social Science Research Council, Bulletin 49, 1942.

4. See G. W. Allport, "The General and the Unique in Psychological Science." *Journal of Personality*, Vol. 30, 1962, pp. 405–22.

chapter six. *Jenny's world: the existential approach*

Do personal documents reveal the true character of the writer? As we have seen, two reasons for a negative answer present themselves. The first asserts that documents tell only what the writer consciously knows and feels. All subterranean regions of his (her) life are hidden from view. The second holds that human nature being what it is, a self-told story is freighted with conceit, justification, and rationalization. On these grounds it is said that personal documents are not the place to look for "truth."

Granted that Jenny's Letters may not reveal the whole truth, yet her flow of perceptions and feelings is the source from which all truth must be extracted. Even if we do not take her self-told story at its face value, we still must accept it as the central cable of her existence, and try here and there to correct, to splice or amend, it as best we can. A person's own story is always (or should be) our initial guide to the pattern of his personality, even granted that it does not reveal the full design.

In reading any personal document we find ourselves accepting parts of it as accurate reporting of factual situations; other parts we prefer to question; and what we see "between the lines" often strikes us the most important evidence of all.

Thus in approaching Jenny's Letters we incline first to adopt the method of humanism (empathy): we put ourselves into Jenny's nerves and muscles and emotions. So far as we are able to do so, we try to view her world as she views it. After sharing her raw experience we then tie together the themes and threads, and in some way form an idea of her existential relation to the world —her "being-in-the-world." Having formed our idea, the question arises, have we also in the process "explained" Jenny?

THE NUB OF THE THEORETICAL ISSUE

It is precisely here that we come to the most crucial of all our questions. At what level of analysis can one best "explain" Jenny?

All knowledge, scientific or otherwise, begins with an acquaintance with particulars. Jenny gives us a fascinating array of particulars. She even to some extent sums up and generalizes concerning the way these particulars blend into her own special world view. The reader himself then continues the process until finally he reaches some conceptualization of her life satisfactory to himself.

If he chooses only to dwell on the main trends as she reveals them, he remains in a sense near the "psychic surface" of her life. He sees essentially the kind of creature she herself depicts. Her motives, like her suffering and her joys, stand self-revealed. The artist and the humanist might say, "I accept Jenny's account of her agony, of her appreciations, of her course of life. What more is there to be said?"

Now, in the main, the existentialist school of psychology agrees with the artist and humanist. The chief difference is that the existential psychologist inclines to read rather more between the lines. Jenny herself, in spite of her fierce forthrightness, was sometimes puzzled by her own nature. Even she knew that there were themes she could not articulate.

> Oh! What is it that is so wrong? Be patient with me—I try you sadly— but I'm *alone,* and it's awful to be in the dark, and be alone.
>
> *(April 19, 1929)*

The existentialist would try to compose, to order, to extract the essence of her world view somewhat more fully than Jenny herself does, and yet would always place central reliance on her own story, and would seek the explanation for her life in this summary world view.

Certain objectors to this procedure (depth psychologists) would insist again and again that the mainsprings of motivation are not to be found on the psychic surface of a life. Documents such as Jenny's are unavoidably defensive, self-deceiving—a misleading ripple on the submerged turmoil of her nature. A milder line of objection (from structural theorists) would hold that the existential approach puts too exclusive a weight upon a person's perceptions of his world and upon his feelings and emotions. Granted that an existential portrayal gives trustworthy evidence so far as it goes, it neglects the underlying dispositions or traits that account for the recurrence of the characteristic perceptions and emotions. In other words, to explain Jenny we need a structural view of her nature. Both types of objector prefer a nonexistential approach to explanation. Their preferences are described in Chapters 7 and 8.

To summarize: the existential approach says that if we know Jenny's orientation to the outer world, to her fellow men, and to herself, we shall understand in a fully explanatory way her essential nature. True, we need to look into, around, through, and between her Letters in order to construct completely and consistently the world view that accounts for her conduct.

To assist the process of existential reconstruction we do well to look separately at Jenny's view of her surrounding environment (the *Umwelt*), at her social relationships (the *Mitwelt*), and at her relationship to herself (the *Eigenwelt*).[1]

THE OUTER ENVIRONMENT (*Umwelt*)

While Jenny clearly appreciates the beauties of art and of nature, and to a degree follows the course of public events, she does not really feel at home in the world she inhabits. *Alienation* is the first mark of her world view:

I often feel that I am the loneliest woman in the world.

(*October 13, 1935*)

Autonomy is another common theme. Many letters stress her insistence upon financial independence.

Oh no! You are very kind to offer to cover a class for me, and I'm sure you mean it. But you see, I am not on my last dollar yet, and to accept money from you when I have some lying in the bank is out of the question.

(October 30, 1935)

From the age of seventeen well into her sixties Jenny sought and held jobs of many varieties, and supported herself (and for a long time other people) without outside assistance. Work was one of her acceptances and commitments to life. Only at the age of sixty-three do we find alienation in this phase of her existence creeping in.

I do not want to work. Why work—for whom, or what? To work merely to keep on going, isn't worth it. I don't want to keep on going. Anyway, I've done my share.

(December 30, 1930)

Persistent *pessimism* is illustrated in the following passages.

No, I'm not particularly depressed—of course life isn't worth living—but I knew that long ago. However, "all things pass," and as my dear countryman said, "Even the weariest river flows somewhere safe to sea."

(June 14, 1932)

What a strange muddle life is, and why must we go through it anyway —of what use is it?

(November 1, 1936)

This feeling that life has at bottom no meaning reflects the "existential vacuum" that marked so much of her relationship to the surrounding world. An existentialist would say that Jenny had a deep need for relatedness and for meaning. (The fact that she constantly raises questions concerning life's meaning with Glenn and Isabel is evidence.) The central tragedy of her life is not her perverse temperament or the loss of Ross, but the senseless vacuum that confronts her.

And yet it would be a mistake to understate the persistent and, for the most part, realistic planning that marked much of her behavior. In seeking jobs, in managing her financial affairs, in laying plans to enter a Home, in dealing with Glenn and Isabel, we note realistic coping with environmental demands, often with Spartan discipline.

As regards the cultural values absorbed from her early home life we note a persistent and unresolved conflict. On the one hand she had sharply rebelled against the Victorian mores and prudery of her family by the age of twenty-seven, and reiterates this rebellion all through her life whenever she speaks of her siblings. And yet the whole cast of her values is Victorian and prudish. She is unreconciled to modernism in any form; her dress is old-fashioned; she much prefers Victorian art and literature; and she is merciless in her attacks upon sexual looseness.

Jenny herself does not perceive this conflict, but the reader, scanning the Letters as a whole, is struck by the paradox.

The situation is similar as regards religion. Jenny kicked over the traces of the family religion and never at any point returned to the Anglican faith. Yet her devotion to hard work and her Spartan frugality seemed molded by the Protestant ethic. Further, her references to God (or to the gods) are frequent, and more often than not, at least semireverent. On the whole, however, Jenny seems not to exist outside herself enough to have genuine religious perspective.

Such favor as she displays toward her environment is directed toward the past. The world as it once was holds her. She is especially pleased with gifts of red roses, scented as they are with memories of Ross's former devotion and savoring of her own childhood in Ireland.

SOCIAL RELATIONSHIPS (*Mitwelt*)

Jenny's social relationships are spectacular misadventures. With virtually every human being within her orbit she quarrels to the point of breaking off all further dealings.

The exceptions are Glenn and Isabel, whose connection with Jenny has already been explained. One reader remarked somewhat cynically that Jenny needed a "crying towel" and for this reason clutched at this one contact. To others it seems that she shows genuine warmth and unselfish concern for Glenn's little family, and that this relationship (maintained almost entirely by correspondence) constitutes her one truly human and normal *Mitwelt.*

Her expressions of gratitude and trust are numerous and in marked contrast with her violent denunciations of virtually all her other acquaintances. Even here there are danger signals, especially with Isabel. Although she ordinarily expressed appreciation for the flowers and food sent her, on one occasion she sputtered critically over a box containing tomato juice, salty crackers, and sardines among other things. She sensed that her tartness might give offense, and when Isabel replied without rancor she wrote:

> Ah, I can breathe again—what a relief. You have written, and you are not blazing mad. The gods are not so bad after all.
>
> *(March 13, 1934)*

On another occasion, as Isabel has explained, Jenny suggested that she come to live in their vicinity. Glenn firmly but kindly took a stand against an arrangement clearly foredoomed to failure. Jenny accepted the rejection and seemed half aware of the wisdom of this negative decision.

Thus in Jenny's world Glenn and Isabel were an anchorage for her insight and for her sanity. Holding to them, with affection and gratitude, fully realizing their patience and trustworthiness, she allowed all her other human connections to deteriorate. It is important to recall that Glenn overlapped with the last of her golden years with Ross and was therefore not involved in her current conflicts.

Highly characteristic is her tendency to like people at first but to turn against them in time.

> There was a woman in N. Y. whom I had known in a way for several years. I liked her. I believed her to be a high-principled, understanding, splendid woman. . . . After I visited my friend a few times, I found that my idol had, indeed, clay feet. She was quite an ordinary person. . . . At once I saw that she was much too fat, her stomach like a sack, and she did not wear a corset. . . . I almost hated her.
>
> *(March 12, 1926)*

At first she likes the Home entered at the age of sixty-three, and its kindly personnel, but soon the Home becomes the "Prison" and the entire personnel villains.

When the mail comes to this prison it is handed in in a bundle to the office, and then is sorted over and examined by the Catholic dog and the Y.W.C.A. ditto. . . . I have always believed (and am not alone in the belief) that many letters are tampered with.

(October 3, 1937)

One of Ross's girl friends she found charming at first, but was soon calling her a "chip," a "prostitute," and later accused her of killing Ross.

While her mounting venom against women of her acquaintance (including her own sister) was monotonously predictable, men came off only slightly better. She became suspicious of all of them, save only Glenn. Following Ross's death she writes of her lawyer.

Mr. Barter is a great help and comfort to me. The administration papers were signed yesterday.

(November 29, 1929)

Three and a half months later she writes,

Dear Glenn, help me be fair and just to Mr. Barter—point out to me where I was wrong, if I were indeed wrong.

(March 6, 1930)

Three weeks later,

. . . am all nerves—and mad as a wet hen. . . . It's all that Barter man—that boob, blockhead—ass.

(March 26, 1930)

A letter in September, 1931, reports,

My dentist and I have had a scrap.

But on the whole she saves her fiercest denunciation for women. Even though she directs verbal vitriol against Ross, it is always women who have seduced, ruined, and ultimately killed him.

Concerning her husband we know little, excepting that she wanted to work and resented being held at home like a "kept" woman. It is obvious that she quarreled with him. Had he not died within the first two years of married life the match might have broken up. We do know, however, that in retrospect Jenny romanticized their relationship and always wore the Mizpah pin that he had given her on their wedding day. Ross once told Glenn that his mother liked fights for she said "they cleared the air." But more usually for her they seemed to poison it permanently.

And what of Ross in Jenny's world-view? He was infinitely the most important figure in her *Mitwelt*. We read,

> The only *real thrill* I have ever experienced in my whole life is when I held Ross's tiny hand in mine and knew him to be *mine*.
>
> *(March 9, 1928)*

This statement clearly expresses love, but also a possessiveness. How often the dual theme recurs:

> Only 1 year ago yesterday Ross drove me to New Haven to the game. Everything came our way on that day—we surely were happy, and *one* if ever a mother and son were one. . . . He did not know the chip then.
>
> *(December 2, 1929)*

The idyll of her life is her particular conception of motherhood. She realized it in Ross's early years when she could work, sacrifice, devote herself utterly to him, fashioning him into a likeness of her own tastes, her own philosophy, her conviction that "art alone remains." The idyll lasted until Ross achieved manhood. He matured—she did not. Jealousy of the professor's wife began the tragic deterioration. The mother–son romance was broken, excepting for rare resumptions:

> He took me to a nice place up here on Broadway, and then to a show —a splendid show—he came to my room on the roof and kissed goodnight under the stars. . . .
>
> *(October 23, 1930)*

Jenny weaves her existence to the theme of *self-pity,* of *martyrdom.*

> If Ross loved me, or even had a sentimental regard for me because of my relation to him, he would never have given his money, his time, and thoughts to a common sporting woman while I worked 12 hours a day, and was so ill—so dreadfully ill—no fire in my room—no window—no blanket on my bed—no winter coat.
>
> *(January 5, 1927)*

To her on most occasions Ross is

> unbelievably unprincipled, unfeeling, and almost inhuman . . . a contemptible cur.
>
> *(May 31, 1929)*

Yet a lingering faith in the idyll remained. After his death she wrote:

> If he knows anything now—anything of the days gone by—anything of our heartaches and disappointments, he must know that he made a number of very grave mistakes, and is sorry for them. . . . I must believe that in his soul he loved me.
>
> *(February 8, 1931)*

Had Ross remained bound by the silver cord, Jenny's world would have stayed idyllic, an industrious and artistic capsule containing just Ross and herself.

A certain *courage* and pathos mark her attempts to rebuild her world after his death. She tries to involve herself in literature, art, nature, current happenings, jobs. Her brief experience at the orphanage indicates a potential widening of her capacity for love through service. But her sense of self does not widen; her world becomes involuted, chiefly around memories of Ross. He was on the verge of reforming, of taking her advice, and of fitting again into her world. Buoyed by this conviction and embracing his ashes she preserved her idyll in fantasy. Ross, she says, is "all mine now."

JENNY'S VIEW OF HERSELF (*Eigenwelt*)

Almost ceaselessly Jenny berates the world and depreciates humankind, particularly the female sex. She blames all her misery upon others—upon her family, her son, his ladies, her associates, the staff at the Home. The torrent of blame indicates a paranoid view of existence, deficient in self-insight, insensitive to her own proclivities and shortcomings. Her outlook is acidulous, abrasive, anti-intraceptive (devoid of psychological detachment), and so self-centered that she cannot recognize that it is so.

And yet there are counterindications. Occasionally she interrupts the vigorous flow of self-righteousness with flashes of self-insight.

> You see, being a narrow-minded, self-centered, selfish old fogey—scared to death because I am growing so frightfully old and still live. . . .
>
> *(February 8, 1929)*

On one occasion she advises Isabel to read Tarkington's *The Magnificent Ambersons,* an account of

> an only son and how a *mother* ruined him.
>
> *(October 9, 1931)*

There are occasional hints of self-blame:

> I am always thinking of him—always wishing that I had done something I did not do—or left something undone, or unsaid. . . .
>
> *(October 23, 1930)*

Such flashes come and go, but they do not anchor her existence. Were they more persistent and more effective they might have led to deeper sympathy with Ross's predicament, with his manly needs, with his problem of dealing simultaneously with marriage and with Jenny. She might have appreciated the problems of her sister, of the Home, and thus fitted herself more agreeably into situations. Greater insight might have led her to see that her accusation against Ross's "old maid" for trying to "buy him" could be turned against herself.

More self-insight might have led her to develop a saving sense of humor. As matters stand her humor is limited to the cynical, the sardonic, the tragicomic sense of incongruity (as in the dramatic description of her disposing of Ross's ashes at Coney Island, October 27, 1932). But she does not really laugh at herself. When there are tangles in her personal relationships she turns not to laughter but to attack.

With advancing age Jenny's nature, as Isabel has said, becomes "more so." Her hatred becomes more intense, her memories of Ross more idealized, her world more circumscribed. Life becomes more of a burden, and despair haunts the dull routine. Of necessity older people become circumspect, more guarded as to their strength and resources, and begin to notice that they are left out of the changing scene. These aspects of normal aging are all present and intensified. Yet to say that Jenny becomes senile misses the point. Senility betokens some loss of faculties or memory or a marked regression. Jenny on the contrary seems merely to intensify her world-view, narrowing it, focusing it, bringing it toward a convergence with death. Her life force weakens, she is tired; but she pushes on to the end unchanged.

TEMPERAMENT AND STYLE

An existential analysis of Jenny's life could go further. Each and every excerpt from the Letters could be used as a starting point (or focal point) for reconstructing her assumptive world. Some analysts would stress her *alienation;* others the *existential vacuum*—the ultimate meaninglessness of her existence to herself; still others would develop the theme of *courage,* or *aloneness,* or *anguish,* or *self-pity,* or "nausea" for life. In all cases, what she herself says—*her* world—is the basis for the diagnosis and is allowed to stand for the ultimate realities of her nature. What she perceives and what she feels are the paramount data for the existentialist.[2]

The reader will note that any existential analysis is bound to add some embellishment of interpretation to her own words. How much weight shall we give to this statement or to that? How shall her conflicting statements be evaluated? What are the primary themes in the scattered record of her perceptions and feelings? Clearly "first order" inferences of this type and some generalizations are necessary in the process of understanding Jenny, even from the existentialist point of view.

But this approach strives to remain faithful to her own outlook. It is not permissible for an existentialist to speculate widely concerning her unconscious; for her world is her present conscious world. It is not permissible to disregard this world and attempt to ground her personality in hypothetical structures, traits, or dispositions. The existentialist remains as close as possible to the phenomenological evidence contained in the Letters themselves.

There is, however, an added line of information that seems to fit hand in glove with the general existentialist approach, namely the evidence of Jenny's temperament, of her vital affect, her style of expression. We quote from one discerning reader:

> Jenny should have been an actress. She was never static nor middle-of-the-road. Either she was in ecstasy, mystically adoring a flower or a sunset, or else she was embroiled in hidden sins, in portentous evil. Her whole life is drama. Her son dies, and lo! it is murder. There are child-beaters; also robbers who swoop down on the still-warm bodies of dead old ladies. Jenny was charming when happy, cruel when angry. Some would say she was "plain Irish."

Such qualities of temperament color her world. Always she is dramatic. Drama brings exaggeration; exaggeration begets hyperbole, which in turn verges upon paranoia. All in all, she maintains a fierce and tenacious relationship to her perceived world, occasionally appreciative, often hostile, almost never neutral. While we cannot explain her high energy it is clearly a large factor in her personal style.

One reader comments:

> Jenny's style is remarkably terse and vigorous. Her sentences are generally simple and short, without complexities of diction or syntax. Her vocabulary is idiomatic and conversational. Like her handwriting, her style is straightforward, clear, direct, perhaps a little masculine (she is described as slightly mannish). The literary style is consistent with Jenny's general style of life: lively, direct and self-assured, resulting from her good literary training and general intellectual vigor.

Her world is always heady, never drab. We know it to be so, not only by what she says, but also by how she says it.

In summing up Jenny's mode of being-in-the-world, an existentialist would surely point to her vigorous antagonisms, to her alienation, to her orientation toward the past even while longing for future death (non-being), and to other similar or related themes—all derived directly or by cautious inference from the Letters themselves.

A MISGIVING

An occasional reader distrusts the existential approach completely. Jenny, he may say, is well aware of what she is doing—playing to an audience. In a letter of April 21, 1929, Ross accuses

Jenny of entrenching herself behind "truths, half-truths, and utter fabrications." May not her letters to Glenn and Isabel be in part deliberate deceptions?

Is Jenny trying to achieve immortality in these communications? Is she realizing the histrionic needs of her nature through the creative act of writing? Is she deliberately recording a myth in keeping with her conviction that "art alone remains"?

Each reader will judge for himself whether the Letters are in any sense disingenuous and contrived. We quote from one youthful sceptic who did so believe.

There is always the feeling that perhaps Jenny was overly impressed with the cheap novels of her time. She swings from the depth of melodrama (the young widow dressed in black at the telegraph key with her child beside her) to the heights of the grand gesture (walking with her grim burden down to the sea where she flings her son's ashes into the waves). She is aware of the dramatic possibilities in every situation and functions as a drama coach, with the result that she "milks" her life for all it is worth. I personally was not surprised to find that Jenny died while making an entrance.

There may be a bit of truth in this pert diagnosis; and yet one feels that it overstates the case. Jenny's dramatic sense is not employed dishonestly; rather her expressive outpouring reflects her very mode of existence. Everything is perceived in high color, intensely felt, and vigorously responded to, whether in daily contacts or by pen on paper.

FINAL WORD

There is no firmly structured school of existential psychology. The label covers a fairly wide horizon of thought. One can however say that since World War II many psychologists have been influenced by the writings of those technical and literary philosophers who are commonly called "existentialists" (Kirkegaard, Sartre, Heidegger, Jaspers, Camus, Kafka, and others). Psychologists who follow this train of thought in America are sometimes said to belong to a "third force" in psychology—a force beyond psychoanalysis and behaviorism.

While adherents to the third force may disagree in detail, they unite on the basic image of man as a "being thrown into the world." Man's manifold encounters necessarily engender personal anxiety because he is unable either to master or to comprehend all the pressures that surround him. To understand another human being one must grasp the other's subjective view of life because the phenomena of his experience are the very heart of his existence. How he perceives his surroundings, how he fashions his assumptive world, what anxieties, meanings, aspirations compose his world-view—all these are the phenomenological data upon which existential analysis rests. The hardest facts in life are the subjective experiences of mortal men. To understand this subjective world in concrete cases is the aim of phenomenology, and phenomenology is the method of existentialism. We employ this method whenever we observe our own conscious relationship to the *Umwelt, Mitwelt,* or *Eigenwelt,* or whenever we endeavor to feel ourselves into another's conscious relationship to his surrounding world.

Since there are various channels of existential thinking some analysts would stress certain aspects of Jenny's being, some would stress others. Perhaps her basic anxiety is the focus of her existence; perhaps her alienation and aloneness are central; perhaps her failure to find an integrative meaning in her course of life is crucial.

Our discussion is not intended as an authoritative statement of any one branch of existential thought, certainly not as a definitive existential analysis of Jenny. Rather it is offered as one mode of approach to the study of Jenny's personality. Some readers will find that for them it is illuminating, perhaps the "truest" approach to an understanding and explanation of Jenny as a being-in-the-world.

NOTES

1. These German terms are employed by various European existentialists. Cf. R. May, E. Angel, and H. F. Ellenberger (eds.), *Existence: A New Dimension in Psychiatry and Psychology.* New York: Basic Books, 1958, pp. 61–65.

2. A simple discussion of the existential point of view will be found in R. May (ed.), *Existential Psychology.* New York: Random House, 1961. An additional (largely autobiographical) introduction is V. Frankl, *Man's Search for Meaning.* Boston: Beacon, 1962.

chapter seven. *Jenny's unconscious:*
depth approaches

Without exception approaches in depth place emphasis upon
childhood and upon the family situation. Since we know almost
nothing about Jenny's early life we are warned to hold our speculations tentatively. While it is permissible to illustrate the possibilities that lie in the depth approach, we cannot make a sure
diagnosis.

All approaches in depth would object that the phenomenological approach of existentialism gives us little more than a picture
of Jenny's *symptoms*. Even by adding first-order inferences we
cannot reach the level of true explanation. The existentialist
might reply, "I prefer to trust Jenny's perceptions and feelings
as a guide. Surely it is far-fetched to think of this old woman as
motivated by Freud's principal postulated instincts: sex and aggression." But the Freudian might retort, "Jenny is clearly preoccupied with Ross's sexual sins; she seems incestuous; and clearly
she is aggressive. How can we explain her jealous and hostile nature except by invoking a blend of these instincts?"

Before entering the Freudian controversy it is well to consider
a variety of helpful concepts yielded by depth approaches that are
not necessarily Freudian in character.

BASIC TRUST

Jenny's principal problem all through her life seems to be her distrust of others. Every human relationship of which we have any record (excepting with her mother, and later with Glenn and Isabel) is stained with deep suspicion. (We have no record of her relationship with her father.)

May we then not assume that somehow, somewhere, Jenny was deprived of original security and trust, without which normal growth and social development are impossible?[1] Possibly Jenny was upset by the family's migration to Canada when she was five years old. Perhaps she suffered subtle rejection after the birth of her younger siblings. It could be that only from the youthful Ross did she receive the unconditional love which she needed. Is there here, perhaps, the unifying theme of her life: a hunger to be loved for her own sake and resentment at being rejected?

Such an explanation seems simple enough to be inviting. Against it is the evidence of her love for her mother and lack of resentment toward her. But she did have five younger sisters and one younger brother. Her sense of sibling rivalry may have been keen. An oldest child in a large family often feels severely deprived and resents sharing his earlier exclusive possession of the parents.[2] When Jenny was forced to become a breadwinner these early resentments may have deepened.

From her sister Betty we know that even in childhood Jenny held herself aloof—on family picnics preferring to walk alone. Whether such behavior reflected the basic insecurity established early, or some quirk of Jenny's original temperament we cannot know.

This approach puts emphasis upon the *distrust* motif in her nature; but so too does the existential approach. Both seem to take the presenting symptom as it appears on the "psychic surface" and offer it as the key explanation. But there is an important difference. The existentialist analysis would hold that Jenny's *current* distrust is the key and that no dynamics of the past need be sought. By contrast, the theory of basic trust would say that Jenny's behavior today rests functionally upon early affectional deprivation. We must seek the "go" in her life somewhere in the formative years. The early constellation of felt-rejection is still the unconscious dynamo that drives her to compulsive and self-defeating behavior even in adulthood. In this sense the theory of basic trust clearly belongs to the depth approach, not to the phenomenological.

A JUNGIAN VIEW

Another line of depth interpretation is based on Jung's theories of personality.[3]

Around age eighteen Jenny's *animus* (the unconscious masculine element in a woman) came to the fore. Perhaps it had always been a strong component in her nature, but after her father's death she was forced to take over the role of provider. When she married at twenty-seven she could not fully accept the feminine role she was expected to play. But soon she resumed her masculine role as breadwinner after her husband died and Ross was born. Jenny was thus not only sociologically but in part psychologically a male. We know that she appeared "slightly mannish."

Jung tells us in connection with his theory of four types of character that women usually invest their psychic energy in the *intuitive* and *feeling* functions. The more masculine pattern is to invest in *sensation* and *thinking*. In Jenny the thinking function seems to predominate. The thinking type likes logic and order and is fond of inventing neat formulae to express his views. (Jenny liked neat literary quotations, and her own style is crisp and well articulated.) The thinking type believes that he is rational and logical and that he alone can keep the score. Ross's statement is relevant:

> Day and night mother recites her own good deeds to her family, her friends, her husband, her son, and how each in turn failed to pay her back.
>
> *(April 21, 1929)*

The thinking type dislikes and fears what (to him) is irrational; tends to be cold; tends to neglect the art of friendship. Hence the love affairs of this type tend to have unfortunate outcomes. And since there is continual repression of other needs, there come outbursts of violence. Writes Ross:

> Every attempt boils down to a horrible scene, in which my various sexual debauches are described in their minutest details. . . .
>
> *(July 6, 1929)*

The thinking type cannot admit that his moods are irrational, and so justifies himself with fanatic certainty. If at moments insight threatens to break through, some convenient rationalization comes to the rescue:

> I can *never* have been a wicked person, or Isabel and you would have sensed it and rejected me.
>
> *(December 17, 1926)*

According to Jung the evil part of Jenny's nature becomes lodged in her "shadow," in her personal unconscious. Sexual desire, rejection by her family, doubts of her femininity, the animus, loneliness, all become fused with the shadow. Since Jenny cannot admit her full feminine nature, her distrust becomes generalized and projected upon the whole female sex. Her shadow sends up the message, "Women are evil." Countless statements attest this complex. For example

> There must be some decent women, even in 1928, but up to this time Ross has evidently not met any of them.
>
> *(August 30, 1928)*

When Ross dies he is "safe" from women, and also from Jenny's own shadow (which she has projected upon womankind). She can now return to her task of thinking out a consoling system of rationalizations.

Jung might point further to the presence of "archetypes" in Jenny's thinking. The great symbols of the human race are available to her, and she makes use of them. She finds comfort and promise of peace in mother nature, in the enveloping sea, in her desire for the cleansing fire of cremation. In these respects, and in her deep love of literature and art, she orients her life to timeless symbols. Here we are speaking of the function of the "racial unconscious" in her life. It is only her personal unconscious that is in turmoil.

AN ADLERIAN VIEW

To Adler overemphasis (in the Freudian fashion) on libidinal urges and on native aggression seems to be a misunderstanding of the simpler dynamics of most lives.[4] Jenny's problem is her conflict between *autonomy* and *sociality*. For a few years the young Ross brought the two needs into balance, but for the rest of her life they were in conflict.

Like many women Jenny has trouble coming to terms with her need for independence. To achieve autonomy and independence one must have a sense of self-determination, of competence. Thus a drive for power is basic in human life. In the case of some women, Jenny included, it leads to a vigorous "masculine protest." (Freud would call it "penis envy.") Jenny demands independence from her family, in all financial dealings, in living alone, in planning her future.

At the same time she, like all mortals, has a lively social need. She craves companionship, someone to love, someone to love her. In her case the need for independence and her social interest collide. After Ross finished college she could not keep them in balance. More and more her social need was frustrated; more and more her independence grew. The paranoid trend is merely a hypertrophy of her independence.

Adler would regret the lack of data from early life. Like other depth approaches he would give weight to childhood formations. In them, he holds, one can detect the guidelines of later development, a prophecy of things to come.

One's style of life becomes established early. Values and fictions develop to guide the course of existence. One may speak in later years of "fictional finalism"—a logical construction wherein one can find meaning for important episodes in one's life. An example lies in Jenny's conviction that at the time of his death Ross was changing his mind about things and that his mistress prevented the process of reformation (which would have returned Ross to her). Her belief was tenacious.

She killed Ross—morally and physically.

(*December 2, 1929*)

She killed Ross all right; she beat his head when he told her about going to Chicago—and she killed him.

(December 8, 1929)

The chip *killed* him, you know—when he spoke of leaving her she pounded his dear head, and it caused a hemorrhage.

(November 11, 1931)

She probably did not intend to kill him, but was carried away in anger when she felt that she had lost him.

(November 1, 1936)

Such is one important thread in her "fictional finalism."

A FREUDIAN VIEW

If Jenny had submitted herself to the couch (an unlikely event), just what early memories would she recover? We cannot know. The best we can do is to point to some lines of speculation which might or might not be confirmed if a psychoanalytic study of Jenny were possible.

Descriptively Freud might class her as an "anal" character type.[5] Perhaps in the course of toilet training (of course we cannot know the facts) she was retentive, refused to "give," and through unwise or over-prudish parental insistence, she may have come to value and yet to fear this physical function and all features associated therewith. According to Freud the anal type in later life becomes excessively orderly, self-centered, fastidious, preoccupied with money and with possessions, as well as rebelliously obstinate. All these features mark Jenny's later personality. The theory also holds that sadomasochism is a further trait of the anal syndrome. Surely Jenny both inflicts and receives suffering all her life long. Indeed she seems to create situations where only suffering can result for herself and for others. Like any masochist she seems in a strangely perverted way to enjoy her distress and relish her martyrdom.

Freudian theory (like many theories of personality) is broadly hedonistic.[6] It holds that "the instincts seek pleasure," and therefore that Jenny's persistence in her maladaptive behavior must give her a form of satisfaction. Although her conduct is inappropriate to her very survival, and therefore neurotic, its roots lie in the basic gratification it gives to her masochistic needs.

Still on the theme of anality it might be pointed out that to her sex was dirty, canine business. At best it was something bought and paid for. In her early years her conceptions of sex and childbirth may have been colored by excretory fantasies. Like many children she may have been shocked when first told about relations between men and women. (When her adult acquaintances told her they had men friends, she says, "I nearly fell dead.") The dirtiness of excretion and of sex revolted her; she wanted to avoid both. Her marriage may have been a product of her rebellious obstinacy (an anal trait), a gesture of revenge against her family for having rejected her. Sexually she may have been frigid. Further we know she avoided all subsequent offers of marriage.

We have already considered the theme of "basic trust." A Freudian analyst would assume that with the birth of each sibling Jenny felt a progressive rejection by the mother. Perhaps her own weaning was speeded up by the coming of a second child. Certainly she makes many references to "oral deprivation." She accused her sisters of starving Ross when she left him with them. She herself nearly starved giving Ross steaks and good cigars. She subsisted on cereal and milk to support him. In her last years the Home starved her. Thus an early trauma of weaning may have fashioned both her abstinence and her resentment at oral deprivation.

Perhaps the principal explanatory emphasis in a Freudian analysis would turn on Jenny's confused sex-identity. It could be alleged that she never worked through the Oedipal stage successfully. Her relations with her father are obscure (why does she not speak of him?). Her mother was positive, competent, cultured, dominant in the family. Apparently her chief identification was with the mother. Consciously she loved her deeply and admired her, but who can say whether some repressed hostility (due to her being partially displaced by her siblings) may not have left a grudge at the root of her later hostility toward all women?

In identifying with her mother she may have taken on especially the latter's dominant or masculine role. There is no evidence that she had a normal, frilly adolescence; on the contrary, we know that by the age of eighteen she was playing the masculine role of breadwinner. Unconsciously she may have wished to be her father so that she might possess her mother as love object.

This psychosexual confusion was not resolved by her own marriage (which may have been more of an escape than a romance). Matters did improve, however, when shortly after her husband's death she bore a boy baby. In this achievement she found some compensation for her lack of a penis and of masculine prerogatives. Ross was a projection of her true (masculine) nature. To be "one" with him, to call him "mine," was to relive her life in the masculine image. After his death she kept his robe and pipe, thus cherishing his masculine identity.

In her love for Ross there seems to be an erotic or incestuous tinge. Their behavior was often loverlike; they "kissed under the stars." Jenny's furious jealousy was fired by something more than his formal neglect of her. Even while she admitted that Ross should marry, every move on his part in that direction released a jealous rage. Ross, she said, must be "sex mad."

And so there is deep confusion in the sexual area of her life. On the one hand she says,

Sex plays a larger part in life than we are willing to give it credit for

while in the same letter she insists,

If I had a daughter I would advise her to marry—marry somebody —anybody—only marry—just to prove that it means nothing.

(*October 12, 1936*)

The theme of a personally confused sex-identity can be pressed further. The penalty for the confusion (dating back to her unresolved Oedipal conflict) may well be a repressed homosexuality. At several places in the Letters we note an impulsive attraction toward women. She starts to be friendly with them, but soon becomes alarmed and fights off her attraction. Unconsciously she may experience "homosexual panic," being unable to face the facts of her own nature. Her masculinity ("animus" Jung would call it) has overreached. She therefore represses it into the "shadow." As a "reaction formation" she turns against her women acquaintances, consciously stressing their physical repulsiveness. She finds their bodies fat, coarse, ugly; she notes their protruding teeth and cannot endure their smiles. (Is it because smiling she interprets as invitational?)

Unconsciously she says to herself, "I love her, for I am a male." Since such a thought would be intolerable to her conscious life, she counters it with the negation, "I hate her; she is terrible." The unconscious reasoning goes further; "Why do I hate women? Certainly not because I (through reaction formation) am denying my sexual love for them. No, it is because they give me cause to hate them." Women, she asserts, justify her hatred: they are repulsive, out to get her money, to open her letters; they persecute her.

In this way Jenny's vicious enmity toward women may be explained, in the logic of depth analysis. Her paranoid trends fit into place. According to Freud latent homosexuality is the usual explanation of paranoia.

One additional Freudian theme should be explored. In addition to repressed homosexuality there may be strong disturbance arising from repressed *guilt*. Having had a strict Victorian upbringing, conventional in its ethics and religion, Jenny could scarcely escape having a lively conscience (superego). Yet only rarely do we find that a veiled recognition of past misdeeds seeps into her discourse. (In the previous chapter we noted a few hints of self-blame quickly put aside.) The virtual absence of self-blame makes us suspect that her sense of guilt may be acute even though deeply repressed.

Why should she feel guilty? For one thing we recall that the three important men in her life (father, husband, and son) all died. At moments she may have wished for their death. Guilt feelings often result when even a casual wish for someone's death is followed by actual death. In the case of her husband and son she may have felt that had she done more for them she might have saved their lives. It is conceivable too that in her childhood she engaged in hostile battles with her father (in order to gain fuller possession of her mother). This memory may trouble her. When she married a divorced man, she transgressed the standards of her strict family. In addition her own sex impulses could engender guilt, particularly if they were of a homosexual or incestuous type. She may even have felt guilt for failing to develop the social, the altruistic, the feminine side of her nature; or for holding Ross too close to her.

For whatever reasons she felt guilt she did not face up to them. Instead of becoming intropunitive (blaming herself) she became fiercely extropunitive. Others are lascivious; other women try to buy their men; she did not spoil Ross, rather he is ungrateful and contemptible. She is not making life difficult for her associates; it is they who have evil intentions toward her. She is blameless; others guilty.

Evidence in favor of a guilt-complex comes from her preoccupation with death. Unconsciously she may view annihilation as a just punishment for her sins. Likewise her Spartan frugality, self-sacrifice, and self-inflicted suffering may be masochistic modes of self-punishment.

Admittedly, repressed guilt, as also repressed homosexuality, is a speculative theme. There is however a plausible case for both. If we accept them we can better understand the strategies of ego defense that mark much of her behavior.

DEFENSE MECHANISMS

In the drama *The Iceman Cometh* Eugene O'Neill holds that a human being cannot live in full possession of the complete truth of his life situation. The memory of pains, of injustice, and of guilt would be too searing to bear. Hence every mortal needs to defend himself through fictions and to engage in strategies of self-exculpation. These tricks of "ego defense" (Freudian terminology) are necessary even if they are frequently incapacitating.[7]

Perhaps Jenny's primary act of self-deception lay in her assurance to Ross that since she was responsible for his existence, he therefore owed her nothing. All through his boyhood she taught him this lesson. Actually, of course, her feelings were the reverse. She desired to possess him completely. She expected him to repay her single-minded devotion. Her exaggerated sacrifices for him were (perhaps unconsciously) intended to make him both dependent and indebted. She tied firm knots in the silver cord.

In spite of the lesson she taught him it seems that Ross did not cast her off, nor did he feel that he "owed her nothing." It is true that his sexual maturity led him away from her, and that he deceived and lied to her. The important point is that she could not reconcile herself to such half-hearted sonship. Unless he could give her more he was to her view an ungrateful, contemptible dog.

Jenny's self-insight, as we have seen, was at best sporadic and partial. At no time does she confront herself with full seriousness of the conflicts described in this chapter. She employs rather the first and prime strategy of defense, namely *repression*. By its aid she keeps many disturbing thoughts from consciousness, including her unwelcome feelings of guilt and confused sex-identity.

Similar is the strategy of *denial*. There is seldom a qualifying phrase in the Letters. She is flat-footed in her assertions, as though she were guarding against any possible contrary interpretation. A telltale instance is her admonition to Glenn:

> Tell Isabel that you and she must never believe that I am, or ever was, just a crazy "jealous" fool.
>
> (*May 5, 1927*)

The strategy of *rationalization* has been defined as giving "good" reasons instead of "real" reasons. Thus, unable to face the real reasons for Ross's neglect she argued to herself that he must be mentally unbalanced and "sex mad." In so far as Ross failed to repay her sacrifices it was not because of her early teaching (the real reason), but because he was at heart an ingrate (a good reason).

That she defends her ego with soothing *fantasy* is seen in her fiction that Ross was about to turn over a new leaf at the time of his death. Had he done so they could have lived happily ever after (an instance of Adler's "fictional finalism").

To a certain extent *displacement* is illustrated by Jenny's attachment to Glenn (in place of Ross). Glenn was Ross's roommate in the green college days when Jenny still felt confident and secure in Ross's devotion. There is, however, no evidence that Jenny displaced her libidinal ties from Ross to Glenn; the relationship was always semiformal.

Another instance of displacement (classic in the psychology of prejudice) may be seen in Jenny's outbursts against "kikes," "Catholics," "way-down-low Irish." Not only does she build up her own sense of status at the expense of these unfavored groups, but directs against them some of her oversupply of hate and aggression.

Perhaps the most complex mechanism of defense is *projection*. This strategy presupposes repression and takes shape through both rationalization and displacement. Basically projection is a form of self-deception whereby one ascribes one's own unwelcome thoughts, wishes, and shortcomings to another person.

We have spoken of the possibility that her wrath against women who tried to "buy" Ross might be a projection of her own guilt for harboring a similar intention. Could her own earlier feelings of revulsion at being "kept" by her husband account for her frequent use of the term "prostitute" in speaking of other women?

The major instance of projection, of course, relates to her paranoia. Never is she to blame; it is always the other fellow. Her guilt is projected upon an *alter*. More intricate is the role of projection in cases of repressed homosexuality. We have already considered the logic: "I don't really love them; I hate them. The reason I hate them is because they persecute me."

There is a milder sense in which the term *projection* may be applied to Jenny. We may rightly say that Ross is a projection of herself. Her life is really Ross's life. She plans her future through his; she relives her life through him. If he has an education, a genteel career, social success, so too would she. This vicarious self-fulfillment was shattered when Ross matured and left her circle of influence. Thereafter she was thrown back upon her own naked and unsatisfactory self.

EGO PSYCHOLOGY

A thoroughgoing die-hard depth approach to Jenny would hold firmly to two propositions: (a) her motivations are hidden in the recesses of her unconscious, and are therefore not apparent to her, nor fully expressed in the Letters; (b) the guidelines of her character were laid down in early childhood, probably by the age of three or four. It should be pointed out that these two dogmas of depth analysis are intended to hold not only for Jenny but in a broad way for all human beings. Unfortunately the information available does not allow us either to confirm or deny these two major propositions as applied to Jenny.

In recent years many analysts have felt that these two dogmas are perhaps too extreme and too sweeping. It is not only the unconscious turmoil of the instincts (in the id) and not only the repressions of guilt (in the superego) that motivate us; but the ego itself (the conscious portion of personality) has a certain autonomy (or relative autonomy) of its own.[8] Thus in Jenny's case a portion at least of her behavior is motivated by her conscious interests and intentions.

To give an illustration: Jenny had a distinctly sensitive love for art and for nature. She could thrill to a beautiful piece of sculpture, to a poem, to a sunset, to the majestic roll of the sea. While it would be possible to ascribe her aestheticism to unconscious symbolism, to archetypes, to sublimation of her sexual needs, it seems more reasonable to say that training and opportunity and native temperament created in her conscious life (in her ego) an aesthetic disposition which we may take at its face value. In this case the ego itself possesses a "conflict-free" interest.

Similarly one might explain her urge for financial independence as a disposition formed out of necessity and long experience. It too may be a "conflict-free" sentiment. But here the depth analyst is likely to shake a warning finger. He would say that there is so much compulsiveness in her frugality and in her preoccupation with money that we should suspect powerful unconscious forces at work, not forgetting that this compulsion fits well into the anal syndrome that characterizes much of her behavior.

Similar is the case of her attachment to Glenn and Isabel. Her relationship seems to be transparently structured. She needs and receives companionship and repays it with gratitude. There is nothing necessarily hidden in her bid for sympathy. The depth critic may counter that Glenn is a son-substitute, and that through him Jenny regresses to her earlier state of security and trust. On the whole the evidence seems to favor the straightforward ego interpretation.

Here again we come to the moot theoretical issue described briefly at the end of the previous chapter. How much of a personality is to be explained by unconscious motivation, early psychosexual fixation, and ego defense? And how much by conscious interest, continuing growth, and manifest personal dispositions that are not merely symptomatic of hidden dynamics?

The position of ego psychology, while not abandoning the depth approach, gives somewhat more weight to conflict-free ego dispositions than does orthodox psychoanalytic theory. It allows for the possibility of progressive development and change in personality beyond the childhood stage, and ascribes some motive power to the current interest patterns of a life.

In this respect ego psychology resembles the structural–dynamic approach described in the following chapter. There is however a major difference. Ego psychology derives from the depth approach and on the whole employs its language and inclines to borrow its insights. Structural theories, by contrast, take their origin in academic psychology. They tend to start with the simple facts of learning and to regard the make-up of a personality as dependent on habits and contemporary systems of interest. In this respect the structural approach leans toward the phenomenological. According to the priority given to conscious motivation we might list the approaches in the following order:

Most emphasis on conscious motivation
↑ phenomenological–existential
| structural–dynamic
| ego psychology
↓ depth analysis
Least emphasis on conscious motivation

We turn now to consider the one remaining approach—the structural–dynamic.

NOTES

1. The importance of early security and trust is discussed by E. Erikson, *Childhood and Society.* New York: W. W. Norton, 2d ed., 1963. Also by A. H. Maslow, *Motivation and Personality.* New York: Harper & Row, 1954.

2. See W. Toman, *Family Constellation.* New York: Springer, 1962.

3. For a convenient summary of Jung's theories see C. S. Hall and G. Lindzey, *Theories of Personality.* New York: Wiley, 1957. Chap. 3.

4. For a convenient summary of Adler's theories see H. L. Ansbacher and Rowena R. Ansbacher, *The Individual Psychology of Alfred Adler.* New York: Basic Books, 1956.

5. This and other Freudian concepts here applied to Jenny's case are defined in C. S. Hall and G. Lindzey, *op. cit.,* Chap. 2.

6. Cf. G. W. Allport, *Pattern and Growth in Personality.* New York: Holt, Rinehart and Winston, 1961. Chap. 9.

7. For a list and discussion of these strategies see Anna Freud, *The Ego and the Mechanisms of Defense.* New York: International Universities Press, 1946; also G. W. Allport, *op. cit.,* Chap. 7.

8. The general orientation of ego psychology is described by H. Hartmann, *Ego Psychology and the Problem of Adaptation.* New York: International Universities Press, 1958. See also R. W. White, *Ego and Reality in Psychoanalytic Theory,* Psychological Issues, Monog. 11. New York: International Universities Press, 1964.

chapter eight. *Jenny's traits: the structural-dynamic approach*

Some psychologists, as we have said, find fault with the depth approach, regarding it as elaborate, speculative, and largely un-verifiable. Better not manufacture for Jenny, they would say, an unconscious which in fact she may not possess.

LEARNING THEORY

These psychologists prefer to start with the proposition that Jenny, like all of us, is pretty much a creature of habit. While we have no detailed knowledge of the way her early habits were formed, we can make some fairly safe assumptions. Probably as a child she was praised and rewarded for taking care of her younger brother and sisters. When she took responsibility, worked hard, and displayed thrift, these actions were "reinforced" through praise, reward, expressions of love from her parents. In time and by virtue of repetition and "stimulus and response generalization" she came to assume the role of a responsible and independent actor in most situations. Her thriftiness and rugged autonomy may have had some such origin.

In her home we know that culture, good manners, Victorian modesty, and perhaps a certain social snobbism ("good" Irish) were valued. Habits formed in this milieu would tend to endure.

Even her rebellion against her siblings could not destroy this familial and cultural pattern laid down in childhood and youth.

Later events intensified and generalized this habit structure. Her husband's death led of necessity to still greater independence. Supporting and caring for Ross removed her more and more from other people, strengthening further the traits of solitude, self-reliance, and snobbism. Since she was not companionable with people, they in turn neglected her, and she could easily interpret their motives as unfriendly. The groundwork for her paranoid trend was thus laid in the progressive isolation of her social situation.

Solitude and misanthropy became for her a generic habit-system. Even in childhood there were "lone wolf" tendencies—for reasons we do not fully understand. On family picnics she walked alone. And now half a century later we find intensification: she turns her face to the wall whenever an inmate or staff member passes her in the corridor of the Home.

When her attachment to Ross (a powerful habit-system) suffers frustration she feels threatened. Perceiving first one woman, then another, as the cause, she turns in anger upon them, and gradually, through "stimulus generalization," against all women.

It is along these lines of explanation that learning theorists would proceed. To be sure, learning is enormously complicated business, and even an expert would be hard pressed to reconstruct the whole of Jenny's adult personality by the formation of specific habits and their integration. Our purpose here, however, is merely to illustrate the approach. (And again we point out that no single type of explanation need be held to the exclusion of all others. It is always a matter of how much weight should be given to one approach or to another.)

A serious theoretical perplexity now arises. How, according to learning theory, can we explain the fact that Jenny's habits persist rigidly even after they have become maladaptive and self-defeating? According to strict learning theory, habits should be broken when they are no longer reinforced (that is, when they no longer yield reward and satisfaction). Since Jenny suffered greatly from her excessive identification with Ross, from her isolation and antisocial nature, why do these habit-systems persist?

We shall need to return to this issue later in this chapter, under a discussion of "functional autonomy," and likewise in the final chapter where we shall examine neurotic trends in her nature.

WHAT IS STRUCTURAL ANALYSIS?

If we say that Jenny's habits are the key to her nature the question arises, How shall we identify and classify these habits? What is the structural composition of her personality?

To answer this question with scientific precision is difficult—at the present time impossible. And yet no approach to personality analysis is more direct, more common-sensical than this. Almost always we think about, and talk about, people in terms of their *traits*, which are nothing other than clusters of related habits. (Ordinarily we use the term *habit* to designate a limited and specific formation, such as Jenny's habit of taking long walks, or quoting poetry, or making trips to the sea. A *trait* is a family of habits or a widely generalized habit-system, illustrated by Jenny's solitariness, aestheticism, love of nature.)

To start our structural analysis we asked thirty-six people to characterize Jenny in terms of her traits. They used a total of 198 trait names. Many of the terms, of course, turn out to be synonyms, or else clearly belong in clusters.

Loose as this approach is, we present a codification of the terms used, arranged in order of frequency of occurrences. Under each of the central trait designations are listed some of the equivalent or related terms employed.

1. QUARRELSOME–SUSPICIOUS
   distrustful
   paranoid
   rebellious
   prejudiced
   bellicose
   opinionated
   tactless
   misogynous
   etc.

2. SELF-CENTERED
   selfish
   jealous
   possessive
   egocentric
   proud
   snobbish
   martyr complex
   self-pitying
   oversacrificial
   etc.

3. INDEPENDENT–AUTONOMOUS
   self-reliant
   scrupulous
   hardworking
   frugal
   courageous
   persistent
   stubborn
   reclusive
   calculating
   solitary
   etc.

4. DRAMATIC–INTENSE
   emotional
   rigid
   serious
   temperamental
   vigorous
   violent
   voluble
   self-dramatizing
   etc.

5. AESTHETIC–ARTISTIC
   intuitive
   fastidious
   literary
   cultured
   appreciative
   expressive
   poetic
   lover of nature
   etc.

6. AGGRESSIVE
   ascendant
   indomitable
   domineering
   self-assertive
   autocratic
   forceful
   recalcitrant
   etc.

7. CYNICAL–MORBID
   pessimistic
   sarcastic
   disillusioned
   humorless
   despondent
   frustrated
   insecure
   hypochondriacal
   fixation on death
   etc.

8. SENTIMENTAL
   retrospective
   loyal
   affectionate
   dweller in the past
   maternal
   etc.

UNCLASSIFIED (*13 terms out of 198*)
   intelligent
   predictable
   incestuous
   witty
   whimsical
   etc.

Having employed this method of listing we note a few interesting results. (a) Nearly all judges perceive as most prominent in the structure of Jenny's personality the traits of suspiciousness, self-centeredness, autonomy; and the majority remark also her dramatic nature, her aestheticism, aggressiveness, morbidity, and sentimentality. (b) While there may be disagreement concerning the classification of any given trait name, the main clusters are not difficult to identify. (c) The reader, however, feels that these clusters are not independent of one another; they interlock; thus her sentimentality and her artistic nature seem somehow tied together, and her quarrelsomeness is locked with her aggressiveness. For this reason we cannot claim by the trait-name approach to have isolated separate radicals in her nature. (d) The few terms marked as "unclassified" seem to belong somewhere in the total picture, although our method does not readily absorb them. (e) While there is noteworthy agreement among judges there are occasional contradictions, such as witty–humorless, voluble–reclusive, self-pitying–courageous. But at this point we accept Jung's assurance that every human being harbors opposites in his nature.

Let us return to the problem raised by item (c). Since the traits as listed manifestly overlap, is there some way of finding more inclusive themes? Surely her personality is not an additive sum of eight or nine separate traits.

We asked the judges whether they perceived any one unifying theme that marks all, or almost all, of her behavior. We received such answers as the following:

Her life centers around the Jungian archetype of motherhood.

If one considers her possessiveness toward Ross to be the central object of Jenny's life, then almost all of her interests and behavior fall into place. In Ross's early years her life was completely unified around this goal. In later life this unity is lost; Jenny then "falls to pieces."

I think the leading theme in her life is the need for self-vindication; everything seems to be constellated here.

Since her behavior is continuously self-defeating I see as central the need for self-punishment, due to repressed guilt.

While I cannot discover any single unifying theme, I would submit that *five* (not wholly separate) themes are dominant: extreme possessiveness of Ross, hatred of women, importance of money, aesthetic interests, preoccupation with death.

Such attempts to discover unity in Jenny's personality are suggestive though inconclusive. Just where the center of emphasis should fall we still cannot say. Yet the fact that there is clear overlap among these diagnoses leads us to conclude that there is definite structure (if only we could pin it down), and that this structure is dynamic, leading us toward a true explanation of her behavior.

A convinced depth analyst, of course, would say that this approach is too much "on the surface," too phenotypical. The root themes, the genotypes, lie completely buried—perhaps in the confusion of sex-identity or other early Oedipal conflict.

Whether we favor unconscious genotypes or whether we believe that her learned dispositions are themselves genotypical, we mark in either case an essential firmness in the structure of her personality. After reading the first few letters we find ourselves forecasting what will happen next. We predict that her friendship with Mrs. Graham will turn to sawdust, and so it does; "The more I know of Mrs. Graham the less I like her . . ." At first Jenny likes Vivian Vold, but we know she will soon become just another "chip." The Home first appears bright to her; soon it becomes the "Prison." Her journeys to other cities start with hope but end in despair. The predictability of Jenny, as with any mortal, is the strongest argument for insisting that personality is a dependable hierarchy of sentiments and dispositions, possessed of enduring structure.

Take the evidence of her stylistic traits. Her handwriting is remarkably stable over time, even allowing for a slight unsteadiness with increasing age. Her prose is invariably direct, lively, urgent, with a sharpness of metaphor. Whatever she says or does she will do or say with vigor. While she is predictably affectionate toward Glenn and Isabel, we know that her chief interest is in her own needs and feelings. Any outsider who enters her monologue is on the distant periphery or else is doomed to be sucked into the vortex of her resentments.

CONTENT ANALYSIS

Thus far our structural approach has been grounded in simple common sense. We have read the Letters, "understood" them, and formed an impression of Jenny's make-up. The procedure is essentially intuitive. The only check on our impressions is what other people report from their own intuitive reading. We incline to put more weight on interpretations given frequently by many readers, but we have no objective or quantitative standard to follow.

Stricter methodologists would ask, Can we avoid such gross subjectivism? Is there not some way in which we can objectify and quantify the structure of Jenny's personality? The answer is, Yes—by the method of *content analysis*.

Content analysis, says Berelson, is "a research technique for the objective, systematic, and quantitative description of the manifest content of communication."[1] Virtually all that we know of Jenny comes from her own pen. As published here the Letters contain 46,652 words. From these discrete semantic units content analysis would seek to reconstruct a more pointed, better organized, and, therefore, more meaningful account of the structure of her personality.

There are various ways in which content analysis can proceed. On the simplest level we might count the separate mentions of Ross, or of money, or art, and from such a simple tally infer the relative prominence of different topics in her thought life (as revealed in the Letters). But we need not stop with such a simple count of subject matter (nouns); we can count also the expressions of favor or disfavor, or of other feelings in relation to subject matter. Such a further step is sometimes called "value" or "thematic" analysis.[2]

Two rather ambitious content studies have already employed Jenny's Letters.

Personal Structure Analysis. Using the whole unabridged series of Letters, Alfred Baldwin set himself the task of studying the organization of the flow of Jenny's ideas.[3] For example, when she spoke of Ross, how frequently was he mentioned in a context of money, of art, of women, of favor, of disfavor? When she spoke of money how frequently was this topic associated with Ross, with health, with jobs, with death?

The method selects, somewhat arbitrarily, prominent topics and themes and plots the frequency of their coexistence in the same context of thought. Also it connects these topics with basic attitudes and value judgments made by her. Since Jenny was careful in her paragraphing, a single unit of thought was often a paragraph from a letter, although in some cases the unit might be longer or shorter. Statistically Baldwin used a variation of the Chi-square test to determine the significance of each association. The accompanying diagram represents the principal clusters (co-occurrences) of ideas and feelings that emerge by this method of analysis. The diagram is based on the unabridged series of letters, but only from their beginning until November 2, 1927.

The reader can judge whether this rather laborious mode of classifying ideational clusters adds anything new to the interpre-

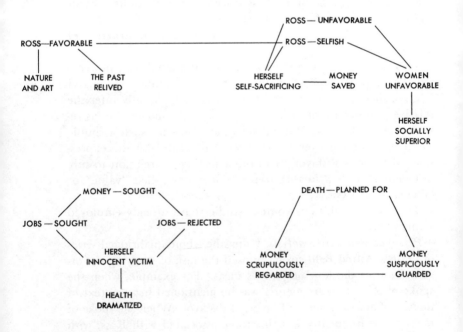

tations reached through a common-sense reading of the material. Perhaps the frequency with which she mentions money may come as a surprise, especially the fact that money enters into all three major contexts of her discourse. It is related to her ideas of self-sacrifice which fall into the ROSS-UNFAVORABLE cluster; also to her search for jobs and concern for health; finally to the context of her death. Interesting is the fact that these three major topics of concern are not themselves tied closely together.

The analysis in the diagram does not cover the entire series of letters. Had it done so we might find the patterns change. For example, mentions of art and nature would no longer be tied almost completely to ROSS-FAVORABLE, but might well form a self-sufficient cluster of values.

For our present purposes it is sufficient to present this brief account of Baldwin's method to show that quantification of the structure of a single personality is possible by means of statistical aids applied to content analysis.

Automated Content Analysis. Some years after Baldwin's study was published advances in computer techniques invited a more elaborate analysis of Jenny's personality. Instead of using relatively few categories for coding and cross-tallying, it became possible to work on a wider base, using more categories and making more complex calculations.

In both methods the first step is similar. The content of her letters must be coded; that is, what she says must be classified into categories. At this stage there is always subjective judgment involved on the part of the analyst. He must decide what basic categories to employ. Jenny's vocabulary is large; she uses many different words to express the same essential idea. A loose woman may be a "chip," a "prostitute," a "sex-starved old maid," or some other type of wanton. What we need then is a lexicon of "basic English" to which her rich discourse may be reduced.

Jeffrey Paige had at hand such a lexicon in a dictionary of concepts relevant to social science, developed for use by the General Inquirer computer system.[4] This dictionary contains approximately 3000 entries which form the initial basis for a coding system. The Letters are first translated into this lexicon, and then can be recast into a smaller number of "tag" words. To give an example, the many terms Jenny uses to express aggression, hostility, opposition, are finally coded together under the tag ATTACK.

The method allows not only for a wide base of categories, but also permits the coder to indicate when each tag word represents the subject, verb, or object in a sentence.

When the material has been appropriately punched on cards and tagged by the computer, a great variety of retrieval operations becomes possible. The program will print out all sentences bearing upon the question the investigator has in mind. For example, if he is interested in Jenny's retentitiveness of money and possessions, he might ask for the co-occurrence of SELF, POSSESS, and ECONOMIC. And in order to avoid retrieving irrelevant sentences, he specifies that he wants only the sentences in which SELF is subject, POSSESS is verb, and ECONOMIC is object. In this way an accurate count of the frequency of this particular ideational structure is obtained.

Utilizing the IBM 1401-7094, The General Inquirer and associated statistical procedures permit coding, retrieval, correlations, and computations. With this automated assistance Paige reaches certain conclusions regarding Jenny's personality structure.[5]

For example, the frequency with which various tag words in a given letter are associated with all others in the same letter forms a basis for factor analysis. The first 56 letters—up to the death of Ross—are employed for this purpose, since they are on the average longer than the later letters. By this statistical method Paige extracts eight factors which he considers to be Jenny's "most prominent traits." They are listed here in decreasing order of frequency.

TRAIT	MODE OF EXPRESSION
aggression	Deprecatory invective, especially directed at Ross and women; anger; arguments with Ross. Indirectly expressed in travel and job hunting.
possessiveness	A combination of nurturant and retentive needs; expressed in Jenny's joy in caring for children, including Ross when he was younger, and in her later attempts to bind her son to her by legal and financial means.

TRAIT	MODE OF EXPRESSION
need for affiliation	Expressed directly by telling Glenn and Isabel how much they are depended upon, by praising them and their home, by writing of the joy she takes in their friendship. Indirectly expressed by exaggerated descriptions of her distress, intended (probably unconsciously) to invoke sympathy.
need for autonomy	Optimism and happiness in being able to support herself despite poverty and lack of skills. Pride in ability to find work and perform hard jobs. Frustrated by supervision, especially during the period of the nursery.
need for familial acceptance	Attempts to return to Canada and be reconciled with Betty, to visit and live with her. Indirectly expressed by associating family values with herself and Ross.
sexuality	Jenny's romantic descriptions of her relationship with her son; rides by moonlight, trips to the country; indirectly by her vicarious sharing (by identification with Isabel) in the affection of Glenn's family.
sentience	Jenny's love of art, literature, and natural beauty. Also expressed by her need to be dependent on Glenn and Isabel.
martyrdom	The nobility of Jenny's sacrifices for others, particularly for Ross. Also expressed by complaints that her sacrifices are unappreciated and bring her only grief, and descriptions of the burdens she must bear.

Although the list of traits derived from factor analysis is not identical with our earlier list derived from common-sense interpretation, there is much overlap and similarity.

FACTORIAL TRAITS	COMMON-SENSE TRAITS
aggression	{ quarrelsome–suspicious { aggressive
possessiveness	self-centered
{ need for affiliation { need for family acceptance	sentimental
need for autonomy	independent–autonomous

FACTORIAL TRAITS	COMMON-SENSE TRAITS
sentience	aesthetic–artistic
martyrdom	self-centered
sexuality	(no parallel)
(no parallel)	cynical–morbid
(no parallel)	dramatic–intense

With three exceptions the parallel is close. It seems likely that the use of tag words binds the factorial method more closely to actual situations; whereas the intuitive reader perceives stylistic and expressive dispositions more readily and thus selects the *cynical–morbid* and *dramatic–intense* traits in her nature.

It would be wrong, however, to assume that the computer method cannot deal with stylistic variables. A special code permits the retrieval of words tagged by OVERSTATE (such words as *always, never, impossible,* etc.). Words tagged UNDERSTATE indicate reserve, caution, qualification. Jenny's Letters throughout the series score much higher on OVERSTATE than on UNDERSTATE. Thus we find the common-sense diagnosis of "dramatic–intense" is confirmed (and quantified) by automated content analysis.

Besides aiding in the search for central structural units the method turns up several additional insights, some new, some old.

It confirms our impression that Jenny's feelings about her own sex are consistently negative (except toward Isabel). Women are associated with the tag words DISTRESS and BAD, almost never with PLEASURE or GOOD. They score high on DEVIATION, meaning that they violate culturally accepted standards; and they score zero on FOLLOW, meaning that Jenny never respects them nor becomes submissive toward them. Her statements about women score especially high on OVERSTATE.

Her attitudes toward men are generally less unfavorable. Her score for AVOID is high (except for Glenn), but there are some associations with GOOD, AFFECTION, and PLEASURE—a pattern virtually nonexistent for women. A close analysis shows that Jenny expresses more affection for Glenn than for Isabel, and makes more requests of him for advice and help. She tends to share her experiences with Isabel but her worries and dependency needs with Glenn. Both, of course, are idealized, seldom spoken of in any but glowing terms. Because she rarely sees them in person she is better able to maintain her conception of their respective roles. Even granted the conventions of correspondence it is still noteworthy that Jenny tends to see people in unrealistic extremes—Glenn and Isabel as all good, others as all bad. And we recall that the same extremism marked her attitudes toward Ross. Evaluative tags of BAD are more frequent than tags of GOOD, but she does occasionally express love for Ross, and once declares that he is a "first-rate neighbor." But among the statements tagged GOOD we find several that are sarcastic—"I have truly a noble son, an honor to his college, his friends, his family." (Let us note that the computer is not able to identify sarcasm.)

Jenny was surely not a discriminating judge of character. It is interesting to compare her personal qualities with those of a "poor judge of character" emerging from the research of Cottrell and Dymond.[6] These investigators conclude that a poor judge is rigid, introverted, lacking self-insight, inhibited emotionally, subject to emotional outbursts. The research discovered further that poor judges "experienced difficulty in interpersonal relations, mistrusted others, were less well integrated, and had had unsatisfactory family relationships in childhood." For the most part Jenny fits this picture.

Confirming our impression that Jenny is given to self-pity we note (by the method of retrieval) that in 289 sentences she refers to herself in distressing situations of one sort or another. Her preoccupation with death is indicated over and over again, more often than a casual reading of the Letters might suggest.

Every reader notes the aesthetic sensitivity in her nature. By computer count there are 114 sentences dealing with PLEASURE or AFFECTION in relation to objects of art, nature, and literature. "I love the sunset over the Jersey hills." "I find real pleasure in our old time books." "One day a customer brought in a lovely nude picture to be framed." Now this region of her life seems to be free from conflict. Even when Ross enters the aesthetic sphere all her associations are favorable. Therefore we discover here a point of considerable importance for our structural analysis. This sentient trait in Jenny's nature has considerable dynamic force, and for the most part it is segregated from the major aspects of her existence. Thus the computer helps us to discover that her aestheticism is a prominent secondary disposition, relatively independent of the central or cardinal (trouble giving) trends in her nature.

Suppose we now ask the computer to examine the allegation of depth psychology that guilt is an important factor. It does so by retrieving sentences involving SELF, BAD, DEVIATION, GUILT. It turns out that virtually none of Jenny's statements seem to be self-deprecations. She does admit that "mothers certainly are a nuisance when they are old, and had not sense enough when young to remember that they would not always be young." Also she states that "I was ashamed, ashamed to have doubted him [Mr. Barter]." But for the most part the retrievals are extropunitive in character: "I always feel kind of ashamed when I see a woman stand up to speak"; or to Betty, "I have always been labeled the lawless one, the family disgrace, the black sheep who married a divorced man." From this exercise in retrieval we must conclude that Jenny consciously feels little guilt; hence if guilt is a major psychodynamic force in her behavior it must be of the unconscious and repressed order.

Automated content analysis confirms our impression of change in her personality toward the end of her life. More and more she concentrates on herself and her isolation. Memories of Ross seem to fade, especially after she casts his ashes into the sea and burns his photographs. To find support she increasingly, but vainly, turns to her aesthetic values. Her dislike of authority becomes more and more intense. She openly insults the superintendent and battles physically with nurses and inmates. Her fury is so great that the Home feels that she must soon be committed to an institution for the insane.

Summary. Content analysis (whether longhand or automated) provides no golden key to the riddle of Jenny. It does, however, objectify, quantify, and to some extent purify common-sense impressions. By holding us close to the data (Jenny's own words) it warns us not to let some pet insight run away with the evidence. And it brings to our attention occasional fresh revelations beyond unaided common sense. In short, by bringing Jenny's phenomenological world to focus it enables us to make safer first-order inferences concerning the structure of personality that underlies her existential experience.

It is well to remember, as Berelson says, that content analysis (whatever form it takes) deals primarily with the "manifest content of communication." It does not directly reveal structure in depth, unless this structure does in fact correspond to the traits we identify by first-order inference—a possibility that the present chapter tends to affirm.

NOTES

1. B. Berelson, "Content Analysis," in G. Lindzey (ed.), *Handbook of Social Psychology.* Reading, Mass.: Addison-Wesley, 1954, 2 vols., Vol. 1, p. 489.
2. R. K. White, *Value Analysis: The Nature and Use of Its Methods.* Glen Gardner, N.J.: Libertarian Press, 1951.
3. A. L. Baldwin, "Personal Structure Analysis: A Statistical Method for Investigating the Single Personality." *Journal of Abnormal and Social Psychology,* Vol. 37, 1942, pp. 163–83.
4. P. J. Stone, R. F. Bales, J. Z. Namenwirth, and D. M. Ogilvie, "The General Inquirer: A Computer System for Content Analysis and Retrieval Based on the Sentence as a Unit of Information." *Behavioral Science,* Vol. 7, 1962, pp. 1–15.
5. J. M. Paige, *Automated Content Analysis of "Letters from Jenny."* Unpublished thesis, Harvard University: Library of Social Relations, 1964.
6. L. A. Cottrell and Rosamond F. Dymond, "The Empathic Response: A Neglected Field for Research." *Psychiatry,* Vol. 92, 1949, pp. 355–59.

chapter nine. *Restatement:*
a theoretical summary

We can now briefly review the attempts to explain Jenny. There are at bottom two contrasting points of view.

INTERPRETATIONS IN DEPTH

The effective dynamics in Jenny's case are hidden because they lie deeply buried in her unconscious. In all probability she is the victim of early conflict involving weaning, toilet training, relations with her parents, and confusion as to her sex identity. The psychosexual syndrome seems to be of the anal type. Along the way a latent homosexuality developed. This unwelcome tendency became deeply repressed, along with other guilty thoughts and memories. Unable to handle the anxiety resulting from her failure to resolve her conflicts, she channels all her tempestuous libidinal energy into a single-minded devotion to her son. Along with this positive libidinal attachment she evolves a large number of ego-defenses to rescue her from the seething id and superego pressures. She becomes adept at rationalizing, projecting, displacing, and denying her fundamental nature. Being ignorant of the springs of her own conduct she cannot, of course, reveal them in her Letters, excepting indirectly and between the lines. Chapter 7 has described the logic of this explanatory approach more fully.

While reviewing the case for hidden explanations we should keep in mind the possibility that her biological equipment is more of a causal factor than we know. It seems probable that her intellectual capacity, her emotional nature, and possibly her aggressiveness were with her from birth. She was Irish—could ethnic genes be a partial explanation of her nature? We cannot say. Could heredity be responsible not only for her intelligence and vigorous temperament, but also perhaps for the peculiar introversive self-centeredness in her make-up, even disposing her to later paranoia?[1] The possibility of deep genetic causation must be borne in mind. While psychology of all types is partial to explanations couched in terms of experience and environment, the preference may rest on little more than our current ignorance of human genetics. When we know the subtler laws of inheritance and their application to the single case, our emphasis in personality theory may alter drastically.

STRUCTURAL-DYNAMIC INTERPRETATIONS

The polar opposite approach insists that the effective dynamics in Jenny's case are for the most part manifest. Jenny is pretty much what she seems to be. We shall now develop the logic for this view.

We start by asking the main reason for *any* human behavior, Jenny's included. Is it not that each mortal person has one overwhelmingly important assignment: to deal with his environment day by day as best he can? (By environment we shall mean, as in Chapter 6, the *Umwelt,* the *Mitwelt,* the *Eigenwelt.*) Of course biological needs, past memories, and forgotten experiences are all part and parcel of the assignment. Yet the task is always the same: to survive and to master one's existential world at a given moment of time. To survive and to master require a sense of self-consistency and an image of what one wishes to be. Fidelity to one's style of being is involved, for we could not survive at all if we altered our habits and our outlook daily.

This line of logic ties together the theories of many psychologists. We name a few.[2] R. S. Woodworth advances as basic to all psychological explanation the principle of "behavior primacy" (as opposed to "drive primacy"), a principle that holds *adaptation* and *mastery* to be the twin forces underlying all behavior. Not dissimilar is the principle of "competence" advanced by R. W. White to characterize the priority in most lives of independent ego energies whose duty it is to relate the person successfully to the tasks confronting him. Adler too recognizes one's current "style of life" as having strong motivational power. The principle of "self-consistency" is stressed as a major formative force by P. Lecky. The fact that most lives are lived in order to achieve "self-actualization" is central to the theories of K. Goldstein and A. H. Maslow. The autonomous dynamic nature of adult interests, traits, and styles of activity is the burden of the principle of "functional autonomy" advanced by G. W. Allport. None of these theories shares the depth psychologist's contempt for the psychic surface of life. Rather they hold that on the psychic surface one will probably find the most valid explanation for behavior.

This course of reasoning leads us to say that the structural approach is concerned not with mere phenotypes (surface appearances), but that Jenny's style of perceiving and acting is itself motivational and truly genotypical. This view recognizes validity in the interpretations offered by the existential approach (Chapter 6). It goes one step further, however, in trying to infer the recurrent habits and traits through which her attempted adjustments and efforts at mastery take place.

The reader may object that we have not succeeded in isolating the root habits and traits needed for the structural approach. The various methods described in Chapter 8 (clinical insight, personal structure analysis, factor analysis) have not led to a perfect consensus. Such is indeed the case, but lack of final agreement at this time does not alter the logic of the structural-dynamic position: if we knew how Jenny was organized we should then know why she behaves as she does.

JENNY'S STYLE OF BEING

From her inborn nature, her experiences, and from the unkind shafts of fortune, Jenny evolved a generic outlook on life. To the outside point of view it is a tragically one-sided outlook. But to Jenny herself it makes good sense. Blending as it does realism, pessimism, cynicism, and a bit of compassion, it justifies her lonely alienation from the world. The brighter of two possible interpretations of an experience seldom occurs to her. A typical instance of her gray outlook is her account of Christmas 1936:

> I went out early on Christmas morning soon as the prison doors were unlocked, and stayed out all day. The Christmas Show at Radio City was just about perfect, all except the admission price—it always makes me sore to see the prices raised on the very day when men want to take their children, family and friends to the greatest thing in the show line that can be produced. If those grafters were really Christ-like they would *lower* the prices so the whole family could enjoy it. It must be terrible for a father to have to leave out little Johnny or May because he had come to the end of his dollars. No wonder men steal.
>
> I was alone all day—never opened my lips to a soul.
>
> (December 29, 1936)

Having almost no human contacts, being defeated at every turn, Jenny's assumptions concerning the evil in human nature and the worthlessness of life make good sense to her. They appeal to her reason. She proceeds to act in accordance with her rational convictions: she distrusts others, rows her own boat, makes her own plans, longs for death, and takes a bit of comfort along the way in art and in her remote anchorage to Glenn and Isabel.

Her style of being is a structural-dynamic fact. The very intensity with which she expresses her views suggests that they have in themselves powerful motivational force. In deepest essence her views are identical with herself.

Earlier we raised the question of how it comes about that self-defeating behavior maintains itself. To an outside point of view Jenny's philosophy fizzled badly. It did not lead her to adapt to or master her environment. She achieved little in the way of self-actualization. We have already pointed to the trouble this failure makes for the "reinforcement" school of learning theory. Jenny would have liked to have friends, but her hostility ruined one potential friendship after another, even with her own son. Yet punishment did not reform her ways.

At the present time no psychologist has a completely convincing answer to the riddle. Why does Jenny—why do many of us—persist in self-defeating conduct, no matter how many times we are punished for it? In extreme cases (Jenny's included) we label the tendency *neurotic*. But a label does not explain.

The best we can do is to offer a comment from each of our two polar points of view. The *depth* psychologist would surely say that he has the more plausible answer. Jenny's self-defeating behavior is due to the fierce tenacity of her unconscious conflicts. Because of her buried guilt she is actually trying to destroy herself. She succeeds in so doing by blaming others (through projection). The result is that she suffers isolation and complete alienation up to the very moment of her welcomed death. This course of self-punishment is planned (of course unconsciously).

The *structural-dynamic* position would differ. As Jenny grew up from childhood she fashioned for herself an assumptive world, a self-image, a generic outlook—all designed to make the best sense she could of her welter of experiences. At each stage she felt some degree of rejection which led at first to normal resentment and normal withdrawing into her own world of values. To handle her situation she developed an introversive, self-justifying, alienated outlook. While such an outlook brought little pleasure (except when integrated into her early years of motherhood), it still seemed to her to be the "best fit" to her existence, and she both sought and created confirmatory evidence through her behavior. From her point of view her pessimistic interpretations were rational, and her way of perceiving the world became the essence of her being. She behaved consistently with her philosophy, because it was she; and she was it. Her hostility became "functionally autonomous," the very heart of her existence.

FINAL WORD

The reader now has before him three lines of interpretation of Jenny's personality: the *existential*, the *depth*, and the *structural-dynamic*. The first and third agree that her nature is pretty much as we perceive it to be in her vivid Letters. The first approach would rest content with a reconstruction of her world-view: its major motifs and themes. The third would look behind this re-construction to identify the traits and dispositions that motivate her. Both would shy away from the speculations of depth analysis, which denies that manifest attitudes, a world-view, or focused traits have dynamic (causal) power. While we do not know the precise forces at work in Jenny's unconscious, says the depth psychologist, we can see evidence in her Letters that the main-springs of her conduct lie there and not on the psychic surface.

Here we must rest the case. Each reader will consider the arguments, weigh them, and render his own verdict. He is, of course, free to decide that truth lies in all three approaches. If he does so he may well be following the path of wisdom. Yet the theoretical challenge remains: if there is truth in all, to what ex-tent, and in what direction, is each approach most valid? Eclecti-cism in personality theory is no doubt necessary, but it is a task for the future to blend the approaches so that a *systematic* eclecticism, a true synthesis of theories, will emerge.

NOTES

1. One study indicates that introversiveness is a highly heritable trait: I. I. Gottesman, "Heritability of Personality." *Psychological Mono-graphs: General and Applied,* No. 572, 1963.
2. R. S. Woodworth, *Dynamics of Behavior.* New York: Holt, Rinehart and Winston, 1958.

   R. W. White, "Motivation Reconsidered: The Concept of Com-petence." *Psychological Review,* Vol. 66, 1959, pp. 297–333.

   H. L. Ansbacher and Rowena R. Ansbacher, *The Individual Psy-chology of Alfred Adler.* New York: Basic Books, 1956.

   P. Lecky, *Self-consistency: A Theory of Personality.* New York: Island, 1945.

   K. Goldstein, *Human Nature in the Light of Psychopathology.* Cam-bridge, Mass.: Harvard University Press, 1940.

   A. H. Maslow, *Motivation and Personality.* New York: Harper & Row, 1954.

   G. W. Allport, *Pattern and Growth in Personality.* New York: Holt, Rinehart and Winston, 1961.

chapter ten. is *Jenny* normal or abnormal?

Intuitively we seem to sense that one personality is sounder, better balanced, healthier, more mature than another. But it is hard to tell on what basis we judge.

Not infrequently two judges (like two psychiatrists in the courtroom) may feel equally sure of their verdicts while reaching opposite conclusions. One reader of the Letters writes:

> Jenny's personality is decidedly abnormal and immature. She is characterized by self-deception, lack of frustration tolerance, and extreme extropunitiveness.

Another writes:

> Jenny is basically healthy. She has a high degree of interest in intellectual pursuits (reading, taking courses, art); a compassion for the suffering of helpless persons such as orphans; keen powers of observation concerning nature and the world of practical affairs; an ability to earn a living and to pay her way; a certain unselfishness even as regards Ross; a marked aesthetic sense; she feels normal gratitude to Glenn and Isabel.

WHAT IS NORMALITY?

Science cannot answer this question. The query is one that calls for the application to human conduct of social (or ideal) standards. The same may be said for all other value concepts by which we characterize wholesomeness in personality: *soundness, balance, maturity,* and *positive mental health.* While each term has its own connotation, it is allowable in examining the case of Jenny to consider them as interchangeable. What we want to know is simply whether on the whole Jenny is or is not a pathological case. Bluntly put: is she crazy or isn't she?

Many writers have presented their own criteria for normality (or soundness, or maturity, or positive mental health).[1] For the most part these criteria represent an attempt to restate the values of the human race, or at least of the Western world. It is true that different regions of the earth and different epochs of time may hold to different standards, so that the criteria for personal soundness are to a degree "culture bound." And yet it has also been argued that all regions of the world at all times agree upon certain minimum standards. It is argued that in all lands an individual must contribute in some way to the cohesion of the group, fulfilling his assigned responsibility, and putting forth an acceptable minimum of energy; otherwise he is classed as abnormal.

It is enough to look at Jenny from the point of view of Western (or specifically American) standards. To guide us we shall employ arbitrarily one list of criteria, derived from a synthesis of many previous lists.[2] In bare outline the criteria are as follows:

1. Extension of the sense of self
2. Warm relating of self to others
3. Emotional security (self-acceptance)
4. Realistic perception, skills, and assignments
5. Self-objectification: insight and humor
6. A unifying philosophy of life

THE CRITERIA APPLIED TO JENNY

Extension of the sense of self. To be mature (or merely normal) a human being must develop strong interests outside himself— and yet as part of himself. A person wholly preoccupied with his drives, personal safety, pleasure, would remain closer to the animal level than to the human. A normal person is not wholly self-pivoted.

On this criterion Jenny does not score very high. True, during many years she devoted herself wholly to Ross; but did she really extend herself into Ross or did she attempt to swallow him into herself? A more genuine case of self-extension might lie in her love of beauty. Here she seemed to find wider horizons for her selfhood. At times too she seemed to lose herself in others' welfare (at the orphanage; in Glenn's family). But for the most part her experiences turn inward and are judged by their contribution to her own comfort. At no time does she genuinely lose herself in outside activities, in educational aims, in recreation, in social service, in religious activities.

In this connection her work history is of interest. So far as we can tell she discharged her obligations to her many jobs satisfactorily. Yet she refers to them only as physical labor, as a means of support, or as conferring or denying her social status. Never is there indication that she found self-fulfillment in the work itself. Never did she "love" her job.

Warm relating of self to others. A normally mature person has the capacity for intimacy and warmth in dealing with other people—at least with selected others. This capacity demands a certain detachment that makes one respectful and appreciative of the other's integrity. Intimacy-with-respect requires that one not impede another in his freedom to find his own identity.

Here too Jenny is deficient. Only with Glenn and Isabel is the warm relation maintained, and one suspects that their patience and their distance from her were necessary conditions. Toward them she expresses normal affection, concern, and gratitude. In accepting her they did not contradict her logic, or argue, or interfere. Had they done so a breach would surely have followed. Perhaps the letter in which she criticizes the box of food sent by Isabel (March 4, 1934) is the most pitiable of all, for it shows the compulsive nature of her self-defeating behavior. For the most part she maintains a warm connection with her correspondents, discussing her problems with them, apologizing for intrusions, and rejoicing with them in family successes.

Yet on the whole Jenny was misanthropic. Apart from her inability to get along with her immediate associates and with her family, we note a general snobbishness. She comments unfavorably on groups of people: on "kikes," Catholics, women in public life, on religious hypocrites, on "smilers." She seems pleased with the playful title "Lady Masterson," for it confers upon her a fanciful status.

Karen Horney reasons that if a person has failed to establish warm and satisfying relationships he will turn inward and "set himself apart"—just as Jenny did.[3] Loneliness, involution, paranoia, may be the penalty. As Jenny grew older we note the inevitable progression.

Emotional security (self-acceptance). Depth theories, as we have seen, tell us that to meet life's crises a condition of "basic trust" must be established in infancy. With this underpinning one can avoid overreacting to frustrations later in life. Anger can be controlled; fears and anxiety managed; even the prospect of death can be faced with equanimity. One accepts one's sex drive and does one's best to handle it with the minimum of conflict in oneself and with society.

While Jenny certainly accepted her emotional nature in the sense that she was always "right" about things and righteously justified all her outbursts, still we cannot give her a high rating on this criterion. Even if we allow that her vigorous "Irish" temper was a normal endowment of her nature, we have to conclude that she handled it badly. She neither controlled it nor "made up" after her outbursts. Whether her early life lacked basic trust we do not know; but her failure at impulse control, her tantrums, and her inability to repair their ravages are evidence of emotional insecurity.

And yet there are assets. Patience is not wholly lacking. Long hours at work, long evenings alone, solitary wanderings through the city—all require a degree of emotional discipline. She does not give way to panic or develop phobias. Her Letters, dealing for the most part with crises, highlight the dramatic moments. But in the intervals she somehow manages her needs and her loneliness. Perhaps literature, art, and her beloved sea induce a certain measure of control and serenity.

We can sum up the situation by saying that Jenny maintained reasonable dignity and poise in her impersonal activities. She was, however, easily upset by threats to her self-esteem, and these she sensed in nearly all her personal dealings. In her human relationships she was not emotionally secure.

Realistic perception, skills, and assignments. In order to cope with life's problems it is necessary to know what the problems are. One must also have enough intelligence, adequate skills, and sufficiently good and relevant judgment to lead an independent existence in one's environment. A psychotic is a person whose sense of reality is so deficient that he cannot conduct his affairs with minimum prudence. If he accepts the assignments of life at all, he so badly misperceives their nature that he cannot cope with things as they are.

In several respects Jenny obtains high plus scores. From the age of eighteen she was almost continuously self-supporting and contributing to the support of others. Few women of her day achieved such a record. She held many jobs, having requisite skills as telegrapher, librarian, saleswoman. So far as we know she left her jobs of her own volition. When unemployed she made persistent and realistic efforts to find work.

All through her life she managed her financial affairs with scrupulous care and integrity. There is no hint of dishonesty in her dealing (unless in hiding her bankbook from the "dogs" at the Home). She refused financial aid from Glenn even when low in resources—would not "sponge" on anyone. Her foresight is apparent when she makes plans to enter a Home. After searching widely, she plays her cards carefully with the trustees of her selected abode. All the while she maintains perceptive relations with Glenn and Isabel, knowing (on most occasions) when not to try their patience.

If her view of life is pessimistic it is at least based on her own harsh experiences, and thus in a sense is logical and reasonable, not a mode of fantasy or escape. Even in her later years she wishes to keep her intellect sharp and to avoid the decay shown by many "old maids" at the Home. She takes pains to dispose of her possessions and plan for her own cremation. She wishes to "button up" her own life with minimum inconvenience to others. Thus on the whole she manages her affairs with remarkable prudence and realism. Confrontation is her style, rather than escapism or overdependence on others.

At the same time there are sad deficiencies. She does not understand the reality of other people's worlds. She cannot realistically perceive Ross's situation or the great contradiction in her own life: how she taught him that he owed her nothing, and yet expected him to repay a debt of gratitude.

And finally at the end of her life we note the fatal growth of the paranoid trend. Her mail was being opened; the staff was searching her room; there were conspiracies against her. In this direction realism vanished; she was developing psychotic fantasies.

Self-objectification: insight and humor. Here we are dealing with the gift of detachment. With its aid a person sees himself as a unique specimen of human nature. He knows fairly well how other people view him, what his own personality structure is like, and to some extent "how he got that way." Most people, of course, *think* that they stand high in self-insight. But do they? Santayana warns, "Nothing requires a rarer intellectual heroism than willingness to see one's equation written out."

It is known that the trait of insight is accompanied by a sense of humor, defined by Meredith as an ability to laugh at yourself and the things you love, and still to love them. Humor enables a person to put his foibles in perspective and, momentarily at least, to check the ravages of conceit and pride. Jenny does not laugh at herself.

Yet in Chapter 6 we saw that she is not wholly lacking in insight. Mothers, she noted, can be a "nuisance" and can "ruin" their sons. On one occasion she writes,

> I am to the naked eye a very respectable, decent lady. Perhaps if some seer could peer into my heart and see the quantity of resentment and *hate* stored there he might forget about the fur and the Franklin Simon lines of my coat and class me with quite another group than the decent and respectable.
>
> *(January 28, 1930)*

Such shafts of self-scrutiny make us wonder why Jenny does not mend her ways—cease quarreling with her son and become "decent and respectable" in fact as well as in appearance. The reason seems to be that self-objectification is a relatively weak trait. It could not offset her vigorous temper.

For every self-accusation there are scores of denunciations of others. She sees herself as more sinned against than sinning. Such humor as she shows is of the order of sarcasm. It is aggressive wit directed against others, not herself.

Jenny's conception of herself does not change during the eleven years of constant communication with Glenn and Isabel. One might expect that after committing some judgment to paper she might think it over, and in her next letter offer a correction and thus gradually advance her self-understanding. Glenn and Isabel were accepting and permissive in their attitude, and made a good "third ear" as does any helpful psychotherapist. But Jenny was incapable of advancing in insight because of the tenacity of her temperament and the set of her world-view.

Depth psychologists, of course, would insist that Jenny's difficulties lie so deeply buried that such a mild mode of psychotherapy is ineffective. Short of thorough psychoanalysis there is no hope that Jenny could reach any appreciable degree of self-understanding.

Unifying philosophy of life. In the course of living most people evolve a set of guiding principles, of generic interpretations, which serve to integrate the successive episodes of their existence. Such a philosophy of life serves the dual purpose of providing *meaning* for what has occurred and a *directedness* for present and for future living. (Perhaps younger people seek more for direction and older people for meaning; but at all stages of life both ingredients are important.)

For many years Jenny's existence had a unified direction. "No woman's life is futile if she has a child," she wrote. There was also sufficient meaning in her vicarious identification with her son—although increasingly her theme became that life wasn't worth living.

The beginning of her Letters coincides with a turning point. She had discovered that Ross had been secretly married. In her own words at that time she "died" and her "heart was broken." From that time on both direction and meaning faded and the course of her life was downhill, marked by a sequence of job-getting, working for a time, becoming reconciled with Ross, driving him away, moving to a new location. After his death she lacked even this monotonous routine; she lived only with her "wreckage."

True she made sporadic attempts to find new goals. At times she sought anchorage in art and literature, but without real effect. Her aesthetic values were not strong enough to integrate her life. She made a shrine of her few possessions, holding them close for what comfort they could give—her pictures, books, Ross's ashes. To a degree money was a cohesive factor. At one point she writes, "There is nothing in life worth living for except money." There are indications that her pride in her Irish heritage (not "way-low-down Irish") was a mildly stabilizing sentiment. And she clung to Glenn and Isabel. But on the whole direction and meaning were lacking in her later life.

There are vague hints that she would like to unify her existence through a belief in God. Not infrequently she refers to the gods, to God. In some contexts she merely rails at organized religion and at hypocrites; but in other contexts she wonders whether there may not be a Power above and a life beyond. Yet never does religion perform an integrative function in her personality.

In Chapters 6 and 8 we defined more fully Jenny's philosophy of life. We raised the question whether her pessimistic, cynical outlook and her preoccupation with death were themselves the ultimate philosophy by which she lived, or whether they were a surface "ideology" echoing the true battle waged in her unconscious. However this particular issue is settled, it is clear that in her case pessimism, cynicism, and desire for death, are not a unifying ground for meaning or a forward pathway for living.

Summary. We have attempted to use a tally method for assessing Jenny's mental health and maturity. On the six criteria her scores tend to be low. Perhaps her highest achievement falls in the area of "realism." Her ability to work, to plan, to save, to manage an independent existence is, if anything, above the normal level—at least for her sex at the period of time in which she lived.

The picture, however, is at best uneven. On all criteria we find some marks of strength, along with many of weakness. For this reason, and by this method, we hesitate therefore to give a final categorical verdict of either *normal* or *abnormal*.

NEUROTIC TRENDS

Since the method we have employed does not provide a con-
clusive answer, let us try a different approach. We ask, What is
the outstanding and central fact about Jenny's attempts at "survival and mastery"? Is it not their self-defeating character? One
reader records this haunting impression in a brief poem:

> I weep for Jenny,
> For her lover's quarrel with life
> And with her son;
> I would learn from Jenny how to guard others
> And myself
> 'Gainst such peril of self-defeat.

The fact that some lives are marked by a bent to self-destruction
has given rise to the concept of "character neurosis."

The essence of neurotic behavior lies in its automatic, compulsive, dissociated character. It persists regardless of circumstances.
For this reason it is maladaptive and runs counter to many of the
values and purposes of one's own life. The neurotic is not able to
work out a balanced give and take required for sound friendship,
for smooth relations on the job, or for domestic felicity. Someone
has said that the neurotic will do anything to be loved except to
make himself (herself) lovable.

Applying this definition to Jenny, one reader says,

> She is clearly neurotic. She is self-centered, self-pitying, possessive,
> jealous, accusatory—all to a compulsive degree. Insistently she accuses
> women of being common and vulgar, accuses the staff at the Home of
> plotting to rob her blind. She intrudes constantly on Glenn and Isabel
> for agreement with her point of view. It all follows a rigid, repetitive
> course irrespective of its fit to particular circumstances.

The origins of a character neurosis are not clearly understood.
We cannot rule out the possibility that, genetically speaking,
certain constitutions are inherently weak and tend to develop
hysterical splits and to lack the capacity for firm integration. But
most theories prefer explanations pointing to poor mental hy-
giene—wrong child training, a failure in early life to confront one's
needs and impulses and fantasies with reality. There is one difficulty with this etiology: not all people who get off to a bad start

in life develop a character neurosis. Many are able to control their resentments and to find an integrative philosophy of life. Not so with Jenny.

Although we cannot tell why, we shall have to admit that in her personality neurotic processes took the upper hand. Narrowness, rigidity, inappropriateness marked her behavior. Compulsively she expressed her anger, having little tolerance for frustration. Almost always she dwelt on the past, rigidly and regressively, explaining all her failures as caused by the misdeeds of others. If a character neurosis is "inflexible self-centeredness," as it has been briefly defined, Jenny stands diagnosed. During her last eleven years we find no new insights, no coming to terms with life, no continuous growth or becoming. She remained fixated on her self-defeating mechanisms of maladaptation.

It would be a mistake to imply that every region of Jenny's personality is affected by her character disorder. Her love of nature and of art seems not to be directly tainted, nor her career of financial independence, nor to any appreciable degree her relationship with Glenn and Isabel. And yet most of the central dispositions in her personality are entangled in the neurotic web.

Toward the end of her life her accusations exceed all tolerable bounds. From the neurosis an actual psychosis seems to be developing. Although ideas of martyrdom and persecution have never been foreign to her nature, now ideas of being robbed and having her mail tampered with represent a dangerous intensification of her former paranoid trend. Had she lived longer her destination is foretold.

FINAL WORD

In conclusion we return to our central theoretical issue. How can Jenny's character neurosis be explained? There are two possibilities.

(1) Her difficulties may lie deeply buried in her unconscious, reflecting malformation of psychosexual development in early childhood. Most likely (under psychoanalysis) we would find a confusion in her sex-identity, unresolved hostility toward one or both parents, sibling rivalry, and scars of rejection; also buried

feelings of guilt and desires for self-punishment—all tied into an anal-erotic syndrome. Assuming that this subterranean fire was repressed, it nevertheless worked through to ignite the psychic surface of her life. The result was explosions of wrath, hostility, accusation, self-vindication throughout her troubled adult years. Her neurosis consisted of her persistent but futile attempts to extinguish the blaze.

(2) A contrary view: Given a certain temperament and intellectual equipment Jenny adjusted as best she could to the situation in her family, to her father's death, to her responsibilities. Some frustrations there were, and to these she reacted with resentment. Since this resentment (to her) seemed entirely rational, it became a foundation for her style of life. At each successive stage she became more and more what she was. Viewing herself as a martyr she continued to cultivate this image of herself. Her character was not set, as Freud would claim, primarily by events in the first four years or so of life. In fact her brief but unsatisfactory marriage to a divorced man, and her motherhood, were probably more important in setting her life style. Upon her earlier habits of independence, love of culture, and resentment, she built the edifice higher. At each stage she lived the sort of life that made best sense to her. The structure of her traits and dispositions and her philosophy of life took firmer and firmer form, as did also her self-image. Her neurosis arose from her isolation—from her inability to reverse her point of view when circumstances would call for reversal or for flexible adaptation. Too much solitude intensified her sense of the rightness of her outlook and her behavior.

From the first point of view (developed in Chapter 7) Jenny's neurotic nature arose from her insecurities and her defenses. From the second point of view (Chapters 6 and 8) it arose from her habits and from her inability to find a suitable set of objective meanings that would guide her life in a world of reality (not in the pseudorational world manufactured in her solitariness). An existentialist would say that her neurosis was *noögenic,* not Oedipal, that is, due to inadequate and inappropriate meanings, not to early parental conflicts.[4]

And here we leave Jenny, together with our attempt to solve the riddles of her personality. Perhaps she would be pleased to know that her tangled life has contributed stimulus and challenge to posterity. But more surely she would reiterate her favorite benediction:

> I thank with deep thanksgiving
> Whatever gods may be,
> That no man lives forever,
> That dead men rise up never,
> And even the weariest river
> Flows somewhere safe to sea.

NOTES

1. See for example:

   Marie Jahoda, *Current Concepts of Positive Mental Health*. New York: Basic Books, 1958.

   M. B. Smith, "Mental Health Reconsidered: A Special Case of the Problem of Values in Psychology." *American Psychologist*, Vol. 16, 1961, 299–306.

   G. W. Allport, *Personality and Social Encounter*, Chap. 10. Boston: Beacon Press, 1960.

2. Taken from G. W. Allport, *Pattern and Growth in Personality*. New York: Holt, Rinehart and Winston, 1961, pp. 283–304.

3. See C. S. Hall and G. Lindzey, *Theories of Personality*. New York: Wiley, 1957, p. 133.

4. Cf. V. Frankl, *Man's Search for Meaning*, rev. ed. Boston: Beacon, 1962.